A Practical Introduction to

The Human-Computer

Interface

Stephen Hill

Stephen Hill is a lecturer in Computing at South Cheshire College and has seventeen years' experience of teaching Computing, Sociology and Psychology at various levels. He has worked with business information systems in the transport and engineering industries.

DP Publications Ltd
Aldine Place, London W12 8AW

1995

Acknowledgements

This book would not have been conceived, let alone finished, without the support of many colleagues, friends and family; and the software publishers who have kindly given permission for screen dumps to be used.

The author would like to especially thank the following for their support and encouragement during the formulation of the idea for and the actual writing of this book: Jo Bawa, Geoff Crum, Mandy Hill and the two Eleanors and Jane Knight. Special thanks to Phil Hart, who first encouraged me to go down this particular road, with unforeseen consequences! I would also like to thank Catherine Tilley at DP for her editorial help and support.

Finally, a thank you to my many students, on whom most of the material has been tested in one form or another.

A CIP catalogue reference for this book is available from the British Library.

ISBN 1 85805 119 3

Typeset by Catherine Bourne, London

Printed in Great Britain by the Guernsey Press Co Ltd, Vale, Guernsey

Preface

"Human-computer dialogue construction appears deceptively simple, yet it is full of subtle pitfalls."

R. Molich & J. Nielsen 'Improving a Human-Computer Dialogue', *Communications of the ACM* March 1990

Aim

This book provides an introductory course text for the Human-Computer Interaction and Interface Design elements of most degree and BTEC Higher National courses in Computing, Business Information Technology and Software Engineering.

Need

Most available books on HCI are either written from a particular theoretical perspective (of which there are several) or are written for mature students on postgraduate Computing and Business studies courses. There is currently no text book available written specifically for the target group identified above.

Approach

The approach of the text is to provide a balance between theoretical and practical content. The author recognises the need to give an overview of theories before getting to grips with the practical questions of how to design and evaluate good quality user interfaces with limited resources of time and money. The book covers the BTEC Higher National Competence 'Design of the Human-Computer Interface', the HCI component of all other BTEC Higher Competencies as well as covering the HCI component of most first-year degree courses. It also serves as a practical introduction to HCI for Software Developers.

The book can be used as a core text to support lecture-based courses, or as self-study material for courses where lecture contact is limited. Throughout there is an emphasis on using HCI to solve practical problems.

Questions

In-text questions are used to allow students to make sure that they have taken-in the main points covered. Suggested answers are given in the text on the next non-facing page. Longer Review and Test questions are provided at the end of chapters, to remind students of the key points covered. Suggested outline answers to the Review questions can be found at the end of the book. The Appendix contains a case study which applies the techniques described in the book to a typical small-scale software design project, and can be used as a model for students' own projects.

Lecturers' Supplement

A free supplement on disk is available from the publishers to lecturers adopting the book as a course text. The supplement contains suggested answers to the Test questions and includes the main diagrams from the text in a format suitable for printing out as OHP slides.

Contents

	1	**Issues in human-computer interaction (HCI)**	**1**
	1.1	Introduction	1
	1.2	What is HCI	1
	1.3	Disciplines contributing to HCI	2
	1.4	Why bother with HCI?	2
	1.5	Usability	3
	1.6	Users	3
	1.7	Tasks	4
	1.8	Interactions and dialogues	5
	1.9	Organisational factors	7
	1.10	HCI and the software life cycle	8
	1.11	Practical uses of HCI	9
		Review questions	10
		Test questions	10

	2	**People**	**11**
	2.1	Introduction	11
	2.2	Types of user	11
	2.3	Claims analysis and stakeholders	15
	2.4	Human perception	15
	2.5	Semiotics and Icons	17
	2.6	Memory	19
	2.7	Human reasoning	20
	2.8	Metaphors and conceptual models	22
	2.9	Social aspects of human-computer interaction	23
	2.10	Organisational factors in human-computer interaction	24
		Review questions	26
		Test questions	26

	3	**Technology**	**27**
	3.1	Introduction	27
	3.2	Input devices	27
	3.3	Output devices	38
	3.4	Interaction Styles	41
	3.5	Training materials	46
		Review questions	47

Test questions   47

4   Standards and the law   48

      Introduction   48
4.1   International HCI standards: 48
4.2   Health and safety at work: general requirements   50
4.3   Display Screen Equipment Regulations EEC 90/270   50
4.4   Usability and software ergonomics   57
4.5   Conformance with standards: conformance testing of software   58
4.6   Legal issues when distributing systems   58
      Review questions   62
      Test questions   62

5   Systems analysis and the human-computer interface   63

5.1   Introduction   63
5.2   The software life-cycle and interface design   63
5.3   Human factors in information systems design: the work of the
      HUSAT centre at Loughborough University   72
5.4   Soft Systems Methodology (SSM)   74
5.5   COMPACT   75
5.6   Participative design   77
5.7   ETHICS   78
5.8   Multiview   79
5.9   Jackson Structured Programming/Design (JSP/JSD)   82
5.10 User software engineering (USE)   83
5.11 The Star Model of the system life-cycle   84
5.12 Conclusions on approaches to systems analysis and design methods   85
      Review questions   86
      Test questions   86

6   Designing interfaces   87

      Introduction   87
6.1   Task analysis   87
6.2   Conceptual modelling   88
6.3   User needs analysis: what are we trying to design, and for whom?   89
6.4   Organisational factors influencing interface design   91
6.5   Use of guidelines and style guides   92
6.6   Tools for interface development   96
6.7   Supporting design   101
      Review questions   102
      Test questions   102

7   Psychological models of usability   103

7.1   Introduction   103
7.2   Definitions of usability   103
7.3   Problems with current definitions of usability: 104
7.4   Acceptance of definitions of usability   104
7.5   User Needs Analysis   105

7.6	End-user tasks and task analysis	105
7.7	Ethical Issues in testing	108
7.8	Goals of measurement and evaluation	108
7.9	Methods of Evaluation	109
7.10	Analytic Evaluation Methods	110
7.11	GOMS	111
7.12	Keystroke Level Model (KLM)	112
7.13	Cognitive Complexity Theory (CCT)	112
7.14	Conclusions on GOMS, KLM & CCT	113
	Language-based evaluation models	**113**
7.15	Command Language Grammar (CLG)	113
7.16	Task Action Language (TAL)	114
7.17	Task Action Grammar (TAG)	115
7.18	KAT (Knowledge Analysis of Tasks)	115
7.19	Conclusions on analytic evaluation models generally	116
7.20	Experimental Evaluation	116
	Review questions	118
	Test questions	118

8 The practical evaluation of usability 119

	Introduction	119
8.1	Expert evaluation methods	119
8.2	Heuristic evaluation	119
8.3	Cognitive Walkthroughs	120
8.4	Guidelines	121
8.5	Other approaches combining expert evaluation and user testing	123
8.6	Conclusions on Expert Evaluation	124
8.7	Observational methods of evaluation	125
8.8	Observation in Usability Laboratories	125
8.9	Usability engineering and metrics	126
8.10	Co-operative evaluation	128
8.11	Conclusions on observation in usability labs	128
8.12	Observational techniques in the field	129
8.13	Conclusions on observational methods	130
8.14	Survey based evaluation	130
8.15	Conclusions on survey evaluation	131
8.16	Practical evaluation: a suggested method for those with limited time and money	131
8.17	Evaluation methods compared: a summary	133
	Review questions	134
	Test questions	135

9 Designing support materials 136

9.1	Introduction	136
9.2	Issues in the design of support materials	136
9.3	Minimalist Instruction	137
9.4	Writing documentation for software	141
9.5	On-line help	148

9.6   Telephone support   152
9.7   Support on the Internet   152
9.8   Animated demonstrations for learning applications   153
9.9   Designing support materials for the older user   153
9.10   The use of full-motion video in training materials   153
9.11   Guidelines for use of full motion video   154
       Review questions   154
       Test questions   154

10 **Putting it all together: the interface design process**   **155**
       Introduction   155
10.1   Increasing importance of Human Computer Interaction (HCI)   155
10.2   Users   155
10.3   Organisational factors   156
10.4   Analysing user tasks   156
10.5   Software ergonomics   156
10.6   Documentation for applications software   157
10.7   Training and support materials   158
10.8   Customer support telephone helplines   158
10.9   Legal issues in software design   159
10.10 Measuring context of use   159
10.11 Input and output considerations   160
10.12 Interaction Styles   160
10.13 Traditional systems design methods   161
10.14 Summary of Interface design in SSADM version 4   161
10.15 Recent approaches to systems development   162
10.16 Soft-systems approaches to design   162
10.17 The Star Model of the system life-cycle   163
10.18 A proposed systems life-cycle for systems interface design   164
10.19 Evaluating Designs: guidelines, heuristics, walkthroughs   164
10.20 Tools for interface development   165
10.21 Evaluating the system with real users   166
10.22 Practical evaluation: a suggested method for those with
       limited time and money   167
       Review questions   168
       Test questions   168

Appendix: interface design case study: bibliography browser   169
Answers to review questions   175
Bibliography and further reading   180
Index   181

1 Issues in human-computer interaction (HCI)

1.1 Introduction

In this chapter we shall be looking at just what human computer interaction is all about, why it is important, definitions of terms encountered in HCI, main issues in HCI and the practical use of HCI.

- What is HCI?
- Why is HCI important?
- Usability
- Users
- Tasks
- Interactions and dialogues
- Organisational factors
- HCI and the Software Life-Cycle
- Practical uses of HCI: using HCI to design software and information systems, using HCI to choose between competing software products

1.2 What is HCI?

Human-computer interaction is concerned with how people use computer systems to perform particular tasks, usually in a real-life work setting (although HCI is just as important in designing non-work products such as computer games systems). The sexist (and inaccurate, since the majority of users were female) term man-machine interface was popularly used until about 10 years ago, and is to all intents and purposes interchangeable with the term HCI.

The following statement is fundamental to an understanding of HCI: *particular* people use *particular* computer systems to perform *particular* tasks in a *particular* context (each of the italicised components is equally important). It is no use designing a system for one group of people performing one set of tasks and expecting a completely different group of people to use successfully the same system to perform different tasks in a different setting – it may work, but it is just as likely it either won't work or will be inefficient.

A brief real-life example might help to illustrate this. Spreadsheets such as Lotus 123 and Excel are very popular application packages on computers because of the ease and speed with which they allow managers to update information. Most spreadsheets also have data handling facilities to allow them to act as a database. But the majority are limited to the data-handling capabilities of a flat-file database, whereas most common business and organisational applications need the data handling capabilities of relational database management systems (RDBMSs) such as dBase, Access or Paradox. It is all too common to see computer users trying to use spreadsheets inefficiently for tasks that are much better suited to database packages.

Question 1.1   Write a definition of HCI in about two or three lines.

Computer users typically fall into three groups: expert users with detailed knowledge of all facilities of a particular system (a tiny minority), occasional users such as managers, accountants, lawyers, teachers, who know quite a bit about how to perform the tasks that they need to perform frequently, and complete novices who have never used the system before. Clearly, the demands of each of these groups will be different, reflecting their differing levels of experience with the system. HCI has its roots in the older disciplines of ergonomics and human factors. Ergonomics has its origins in the need for efficient design of interfaces between humans and complex machinery such as aircraft and motor vehicles. Originally, ergonomists concerned themselves solely with physical aspects of design, but soon realised it was necessary to also include psychological (cognitive) and sociological aspects as well.

1.3 Disciplines contributing to HCI

The main disciplines contributing to HCI include:

- Ergonomics- the study of the design of work
- Computer science
- Psychology
- Sociology
- Software engineering
- Design

This list isn't necessarily exhaustive, but each of the above have made significant contributions to HCI.

Question 1.2   Draw a simple diagram to show how you think the different disciplines that contribute to HCI are related to the definition of HCI that you produced in question 1.1.

1.4 Why bother with HCI?

The 1970s and 80s held out the prospect of big increases in productivity as a result of the introduction of computers. However, a US study in the late 1980s (Eason 1988) found that in only 20% of the systems studied was the new system judged a success, with 40% producing only marginal gains and 40% resulting in failure or rejection of the system. The following examples illustrate some of the deficiencies in everyday systems, and some of the costs in cash, stress, time and frustration. They are all caused by HCI problems.

- In the late 1960s a US university decided to computerise its student registration system. It was estimated it would take 3 years to develop, require 20 operators during the registration period and cost $330,000. The system was eventually brought on-line 4 years late in 1975, at a cost of $1,500,000 (5 times over budget) and needing 30 operators. Under the old system, registration took just under one hour, under the new system, nine hours! When senior managers went to look at what was happening they were spat upon by the waiting students. The director of student registration had a nervous breakdown and lost his job.

- In the early 1990s, a work colleague of one of the author's students was hauled before her manager over her poor work performance and given warnings of the need to improve or face the sack. Subsequently the poor performance was traced to bugs in the system.

- In the 1980s there were several air crashes involving a particular type of aircraft, often with hundreds of fatalities. In several cases the crash was attributed to the pilot making a mistake in his interpretation of the instrument readings or controls, thereby plunging the aircraft to the ground.

- Try asking your grandparents to programme the video to record a couple of TV programmes or to adjust the time when the clocks go back on your digital watch?

- Many computer users have seen the 'Keyboard error: no keyboard detected, press any key to continue' message on their screens, leaving them more than a little confused.

There is also evidence that there is money to be made in HCI. The success of the Apple Macintosh range of computers in the 1980s was based on their ease of use for non-computing experts. They managed to maintain an approximately 7% share of the market for personal computers and a higher margin of profitability than their rivals. Similarly the software company Microsoft has been enormously successful since it devoted its efforts to producing software that had higher levels of usability such as Windows, Word for Windows, Excel and Access, than its rivals' products.

Question 1.3   Give brief reasons why developers should bother with HCI.

1.5 Usability

Usability is central to the human-computer interface, since the whole point of interface design is to produce systems that are easy to learn and which allow users to work efficiently, effectively and comfortably. The International Standards Organisation (ISO) are currently working on usability standards for software, and we explore usability further in chapters seven and eight.

1.6 Users

We can divide users of any computer system into the following broad categories:

- **Expert users.** People with in-depth knowledge of the system who use it virtually all the time. They are not necessarily computer specialists, but know the system inside out. For example, an experienced secretary who had been using the same wordprocessor for five years.

Answer 1.1   *Your definition will probably focus on how particular users use computers to perform particular tasks, in a particular setting, and that not all users are alike but fall into categories such as novice, occasional or expert user.*

Answer 1.2   *A possible diagram is the one shown below.*

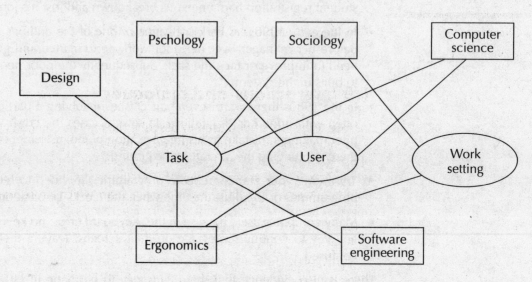

Answer 1.3   *The commercial success of those companies that have embraced interface factors show that there is money in good interface design.*

- **Novice users.** We are all in this category at some stage. Those who haven't used the system at all before, or only very superficially. For example, computing students who haven't used a particular package before.

- **Occasional users** – the vast majority of us. Such users often use a system quite regularly, but only for a limited range of tasks. Occasional users can be like experts for that range of tasks, but like novices for all other tasks.

- **Users with special needs.** Many users with severe disabilities successfully use computer systems that have been specially adapted, for example blind users can use speech recognition and speech synthesis to enable them to use computers.

Question 1.4   Briefly distinguish between the main types of computer system user.

1.7 Tasks

Poor task design can cause stress in employees, lowering their effectiveness, efficiency and motivation. Stress can also cause serious health problems; we are probably all familiar with tales of fellow employees having a breakdown or taking ill-health retirement because their jobs became too much for them. In late 1994 a UK employee successfully won an action for stress against his employer, establishing the precedent that a job which is designed in such a way as to cause stress in an individual breaks the legal requirement for employers to provide a safe system of work.

Tasks should be designed to offer users variety, chances to exercise discretion, training opportunities and should provide feedback. Routine repetitive and boring tasks should be re-designed to increase variety. Adequate staffing levels should be maintained to cope with the volume of work, and end-users should be involved in the planning and design of information systems.

Question 1.5   Why should employers be concerned with task design?

1.8 Interactions and dialogues

Various terms have been used to describe the human-computer interface. Since there is a sequence of user actions followed by responses from their computer, we can think of using a computer as an *interaction* between the user (or users in the case of group-working or other shared systems) and the computer. Similarly, we can think of computer use as involving a *dialogue*, a term which arose when most interactions between users and computers took place on text-only terminals. Nowadays, the term dialogue is still often used, even though the interaction may involve graphics and icons as well as or instead of text.

Early interaction styles between users and computers were very different from those we take for granted today. In the early 1970s, virtually all processing was batch processing and was non-interactive. If for example, a user wanted to run a statistics program to see if an experimental result was significant, they would have to prepare the data on punched cards (or have some keypunch operators prepare the data for them). The cards would then be sent to the data processing clerks, who would arrange for the data to be processed. Several days later the user could pick up a printout of the results of the test. In this era, no-one worried much about interface design, since the end-users didn't actually use computers themselves, rather data preparation clerks and computer operators actually prepared and ran the programs. In such an environment, there was no real need to consider software ergonomics since all users could be assumed to be highly trained computer operators.

Early interactive on-line processing systems started to become available during the 1970s. Initially, users had no access to VDUs but instead had to use Teletype terminals. These were like large electro-mechanical typewriters on which commands were typed which were then run by the computer. Clearly no graphics facilities were available. The Teletype also incorporated a printer. The user would see their commands printed on the paper roll as they typed, and the results of their instructions would similarly be output to the teletype.

By the mid to late 1970s VDUs started to become commonplace and the first standalone personal computers started to appear, such as the Commodore PET. The VDUs were text-only, but allowed faster input and output than the old teletype terminals. When using such terminals, the only text editors available initially were line editors, which didn't allow movement around the whole screen, but only backwards and forwards along the current line, rather like the EDLIN editor supplied with versions of MS-DOS up to version 4.

Question 1.6   What are the differences between the terms dialogue, interaction, interface design and HCI design?

Answer 1.4

Novice users have no knowledge of the system. Expert users use it routinely and know most of the system. Occasional users are like experts for a limited range of tasks, but like novices for all other tasks.

Answer 1.5

Because poorly designed tasks lower productivity and increase levels of absenteeism and staff turnover. They also make the employer liable to be sued for damaging employees health and for breaching health and safety at work legislation.

Answer 1.6

These terms are largely interchangeable with one another. The term dialogue design came about at a time when most systems were text-based rather than graphical, but can be used for graphical systems.

Up to this time, the only interfaces available were command-language interfaces, where precise, syntactically correct commands had to be entered, rather like commands in UNIX or MS-DOS. Whilst some such commands were intuitive and easy to remember, such as SAVE, others were less so, such as ! in dBase IV, which was the command to run a DOS command, or CTRL-J in VAX/VMS to delete the word to the left of the cursor. The accidental inclusion of an extra space, or even typing the command in the wrong case, or the addition or omission of a punctuation mark, would make the command fail. Furthermore, there was no standardisation of commands, so the command to perform the same or similar operation could be completely different in different applications, for example, the command to insert a date in WordPerfect for DOS deletes a block of text in WordStar for DOS.

Question 1.7

Try to find some examples of such inconsistencies across different packages. Why are they a problem?

By the late 1970s researchers in cognitive science had discovered that if commands were displayed in menus for the user to choose from, rather than having to remember the correct syntax etc. , users were better able to recognise the correct command. Furthermore, selecting the command from a menu avoided the possibility of spelling or syntactic mistakes and saved a few keystrokes. More and more novice or occasional users started to use computers, and recall of correct commands was a problem for such users. As a result, menu-driven interfaces started to become popular.

However, experienced users found that working with menus was a lot slower than entering the (cryptic) keystrokes that they had committed to memory. Typically, it takes 10 times as long to point to a menu item with a mouse as to enter a keystroke. To overcome this problem, packages started to offer the facility to turn the menus off and to allow experienced users to carry-on using the keystroke shortcuts. Perhaps the best example of such an approach is the wordprocessor WordStar, whose current version 2.0 for Windows retains keystroke compatibility with the mid-1980s version 3.3 for DOS.

The adoption of menus occurred before widespread availability of mice, so menu items were chosen using cursor movement keys, with the menus themselves typically being dropped-down by a combination of the ALT key and the first letter of the menu, for example ALT-F to drop down the File menu. The widespread introduction of mice in the late 1980s allowed users to point to menu items and select them with the mouse.

The emergence of graphics terminals in the 1980s allowed the development of direct-manipulation WIMP environments such as GEM, Windows and the Apple Macintosh. These allowed the simultaneous display of different parts of a file, or even different files or applications; the use of icons to represent items and actions such as files, folders, waste-baskets, printers etc.; and the use of mice or other pointing devices to drag (directly manipulate) objects on-screen.

The late 1980s and early 1990s have seen the development of speech and tactile interaction styles, with the output of synthesised speech, the development of commercial voice recognition systems that can accept normal speech, such as the Philips and dragon Dictate systems, and the development of data gloves which can be used to manipulate 3-dimensional objects. December 1994 saw the UK marketing of home virtual reality headsets and games software.

Question 1.8

Distinguish between direct manipulation and menu-based dialogue styles.

A further important class of new interaction styles are those designed to support group working, in particular the video conferencing and shared whiteboard systems such as Intel Proshare. Such systems allow several participants to share access to an electronic whiteboard which is displayed on each participants VDU, along with video images of the other participants. Such systems require ISDN telephone lines and PCs equipped with miniature video cameras.

Question 1.9

What possible implications are there for a company introducing video conferencing systems?

1.9 Organisational factors

Up to the early 1970s, most computer systems were simply replacing existing manual systems. Users of computers were highly trained specialists, and computing power was a very scarce and expensive resource. Most western economies enjoyed nearly full employment and rising living standards. Against such a background, computerisation was perceived very differently from the way it is perceived today. Employees were unlikely to feel that their jobs were threatened, and even if they were plenty of other jobs were available. Computerisation was presented as job-enriching, making work more satisfying and enjoyable. Since systems usually replaced clearly-defined existing manual systems, there was no need to determine system requirements.

Since so few people actually worked with computers, issues of threats to managers' control and authority didn't really arise, as such effects hadn't been experienced at that time; indeed computers held out the promise of extending managerial control, and organisations were largely seen as having a clearly defined set of goals which were accepted by all concerned rather than as sites of conflict between competing groups.

However, experience of computerisation and changes to the economy and society during the 1970s and 80s have changed this rather rosy picture of computerisation. The high levels of system failure, with up to 80% of systems producing either no or only marginal benefits; large-scale job losses amongst employees in sectors such as banking and insurance as a direct result of computerisation; the background of high levels of unemployment generally, and the use of systems to serve new functions such as management information systems and decision support, together with much more

Answer 1.7

You could come up with lots of examples for this. Alternatively, there is sometimes a high degree of consistency across applications, for example many text editors use the same keystrokes to perform the same functions as those used by WordStar. examples include the Borland Turbo Pascal editors, the dBase editor and the DR-DOS editor.

Answer 1.8

Direct manipulation interfaces are ones where objects are selected and dragged to perform actions, such as drag and drop text editing in Word for Windows, or the movement and copying of files in the Windows 3.1 File Manager. Menu-based interfaces involve selecting items with either keystrokes or mice, but no dragging of objects.

Answer 1.9

Video conferencing systems could be opposed by potential users who enjoy travelling to conventional meetings, particularly if such conventional conferences and travel are seen as part of the perks of the job. They could also increase the intensity of work since the time formerly spent travelling could be used more productively. On the other hand, the time savings may allow participants to complete their work in less time, work shorter hours, and even work from home rather than commuting to work.

widespread computer literacy have all meant that employees are now much more ready to question the effects of computerisation.

Organisational analysts have found that rather than most organisations having a shared consensus as to what the organisation's goals are and how best to achieve them, instead most organisations are characterised by different interest groups in conflict with each other, even where there is agreement on the organisation's goals. Any change, including computerisation has been shown to bring instability to organisations just by virtue of the fact that it is likely to upset existing power relationships within organisations. Against such a background, the design and evaluation of new computer systems has to take account of the characteristics of the organisational environment in which it occurs. Narrow approaches to evaluation which ignore such contextual factors are unlikely to be able to predict and explain the success of a particular system or systems.

Question 1.10

Why do we need to take organisational factors into account when designing systems?

1.10 HCI and the software life cycle

Since the 1970s, structured approaches to computer systems development have been the norm. Structured methods arose in response to the need to control computer projects, which typically over-ran both their time and budget by factors of several hundred percent. In addition, advances in software engineering and the adoption of the notion of structured programming meant the demise of the unstructured, 'spaghetti' code approach to writing programs of the 1960s.

Structured methods in the 1970s adopted the 'waterfall' model of development, where the project was divided into separate stages of Requirements analysis, Logical design, Physical design, Implementation and Testing. Each stage was subdivided into a number of tasks, with all tasks from one stage being completed prior to moving on to the next stage. Such an approach allowed careful project planning, and the establishment of system requirements formed the basis for a contract between the system developers, and the client, the aim being to ensure that everybody knew just what was supposed to be delivered, in what time scale. Such an approach generally had little to say about interface design, since most projects involved computerisation of existing manual systems, with relatively small numbers of highly trained users. It was generally assumed that computerising the functionality of the manual system was all that was required, with the relatively few users of the new system being trained in the (usually command- language) interface. Examples of such structured methods include those such as JSP/JSD, Gane and Sarson, Yourdon and Constantine, and SSADM.

Advances in both hardware and software, together with the emergence of new types of computers (personal, standalone PCs) and new types of user (novice and occasional users, with no computing background) lead to demands for easier to understand and use interfaces in the 1980s. Software application vendors found that most products in a particular category, such as wordprocessors or spreadsheets, had more than enough functionality for the vast majority of their users, and a few companies, notably Apple with its Macintosh range of computers, decided to develop systems that were easier to learn and use rather than keeping on adding new and unnecessary additional functionality to software.

The realisation of the importance of designing systems for these new types of users on the new types of personal computer meant that traditional methods of systems development had to be modified to include the design and evaluation of the interface at a stage in development where it was possible to influence the design of the product, rather than trying to 'bolt-on' an interface to an already finished product. To meet these interface design requirements, some methods were modified to incorporate interface design stages, for example SSADM version 4, and other new methods appeared, such as COMPACT and Multiview. To date, though, there is no accepted standard method for the development of systems that incorporates human-computer interface design and evaluation principles satisfactorily.

Question 1.11　　Why have traditional approaches to systems design had so little to say concerning the design of the interface?

1.11 Practical uses of HCI

We conclude this chapter by looking at some practical aspects of HCI. As we've seen earlier, there is evidence to suggest that many computer systems fail to live up to their promises and to be difficult or nearly impossible to use. A bottom line measure of the usability of computer systems is to see whether they are actually used at all, since the worst systems are simply abandoned, either officially or unofficially.

HCI is bound to become more important over the next few years as it will become a legal requirement, under European Union health and safety at work directives that software is easy to use and provides adequate feedback to users.

HCI will be increasingly important in he following areas:

- as part of the software development process and systems design methods
- as part of future legal requirements for software

Answer 1.10

We can't simply assume that organisations have clear goals that all agree to, let alone that there is agreement as to how to achieve those goals. An individual who is particularly unpopular may find intense opposition to anything they try to introduce, on purely personal grounds. We should expect to find conflict as a norm in most organisations. Systems which ignore such conflicts and power relationships are unlikely to succeed.

Answer 1.11

Partly this is because the kinds of systems being computerised, and the socio-economic context, were so very different in the 1960s and early 70s. More recent methods have tried to incorporate HCI considerations, but as we have seen, many developers are themselves unsure just what usability is and how to achieve it.

- as the basis for a set of usability criteria to evaluate and choose from amongst competing products

- as the basis for a successful marketing strategy to the increasingly important home and small business user

In future, when an organisation is considering upgrading its wordprocessor, spread-sheet or other application, it is likely to place greater emphasis on usability than in the past, since functionality differs little between the main products in each category, and it is usability that will ultimately determine productivity and costs of upgrading.

The success of companies such as Apple and Microsoft, who have placed the emphasis on usability, together with initiatives such as the UK-government 'Usability Now' initiative of the early 1990s, have all shown that usability isn't just a desirable but non-essential feature of computer systems, but that it makes sound commercial sense. Developments in systems for those with special needs has shown that usability can help to integrate them into normal work environments on more or less equal terms with other users.

Review questions

1. How is usability related to HCI?

2. What do HCI experts mean when they talk about tasks?

3. Why do systems designers need to study the people in organisations?

4. What different types of users do designers need to consider?

Test question

How have interaction styles changed since the late 1970s?

2 People

2.1 Introduction

In this chapter we will be covering the human factors that are important in the design of interfaces. We will briefly discuss the different types of computer users, then go on to look at psychological factors such as perception and memory that affect how we relate to and use interfaces. Finally we shall look at social and organisational factors affecting computer systems and interface design.

- Types of user
- Human perception
- Human memory
- Human reasoning
- Metaphors and conceptual models
- Social aspects of HCI
- Organisational factors and HCI
- Context of use of systems

2.2 Types of user

We can categorise users into the following broad groupings:

- Novice
- Expert
- Occasional
- The 'older' user
- Users with special needs
- Group workers: Computer Supported Co-operative Work (CSCW)

We also need to consider general factors such as level of education, and experience with computers and other software, since for example someone who has used text-based spreadsheets extensively but who has never used a windows product like Excel will clearly be at an advantage compared to someone with no prior experience of using spreadsheets.

2.2.1 Novice users

These are people who have never used the application before, or have only used it very briefly (however, they may have extensive experience of similar applications). We are all novices at some stage. Novices need to be able to learn how to perform necessary tasks as quickly as possible in ways that sustain their motivation to use the software.

Novices benefit from the use of menus since it is much easier to *recognise* a particular command and select it from a menu than it is to *recall* the exact command in a command language interface. For example it is easier to select the File menu and then select Save than it is to remember a command such as 'Save mydoc.doc A:'.

Don't forget that people need to be trained how to use mice, and how to click and double click etc.

For novice users, it is particularly important to design suitable training materials, a topic we cover in more depth in Chapter 9.

2.2.2 Experts

Experts are thoroughly familiar with the software and use it extensively. Data entry workers, word processor operators etc. fall into the expert category. For experts, speed and efficiency are the main requirements. They usually want keystroke shortcuts for commonly performed actions, since such users (particularly those from a typing or secretarial background) often find using mice quite slow compared to keyboarding (an experienced typist takes on average 0.12 seconds to press a key compared with 1.1 seconds to point at something with a mouse-nine times as long). When designing interfaces for experts it is necessary to work out what actions they perform frequently and provide keystroke shortcuts. Most packages have long lists of difficult to remember keystrokes for such purposes, and many allow you to customise the package using macros to perform almost any combination of actions. Most word processors make extensive use of the function keys, either on their own or in combination with the Shift, ALT and CTRL keys, to perform 40-60 common operations such as changing the case of text, accessing help, printing, saving etc.

Exercise

Use a **windows** word processor to open a multi-page document. Move from the beginning to the end using the mouse and scroll bars, then move the cursor back to the beginning of the document. Now use help to find the keystroke shortcuts to move to the end and beginning of documents. Much quicker, isn't it? Imagine you had typed all of the first page in capitals, when it should have been in lower case. See if there is a quick way to change the case of the whole page.

It can be difficult to make software easy to use for both novices and experts since features that help novices such as extensive use of mice and menus can slow down the expert user. Ideally, it should be possible for expert users to customise the interface rather than having to continue to use relatively inefficient procedures. Similarly the kind of help systems required by expert users will be different from those suitable for novices.

2.2.3 Occasional users

Occasional users are those, such as teachers, managers, lawyers etc. who use an application to do certain things, without ever becoming experts in the use of all the facilities of the package. How should we design software for such users? Evidence suggests that such occasional users are like experts for the limited range of tasks that they use the software for, but like novices for the rest of the software's features, and that they aren't usually interested either in learning more about the package or in discovering more efficient methods to perform the tasks that they use the software for, preferring instead to stick with their sub-optimal strategies that nevertheless get the job done. In a nutshell, we don't really need to consider such users separately from the expert and novice categories, just to acknowledge that they behave in the ways described. Since working with the software is not their main work activity anyway, it is less important for them to use software optimally.

2.2.4 The older user

Older users of computers are likely to become more important as the average age of the population increases in most industrialised societies. Estimates for the USA suggest a 50% increase in numbers over 55 in the work force between 1990 and 2005. Since it is only in the last decade or so that computers have been widespread in the education system, there are still many adults who lack computer literacy and experience, yet computer use, both at work and outside, is bound to increase.

- The elderly suffer a decline in short term memory performance and reaction time with age, so tasks should avoid either of these wherever possible

- Older users often suffer from a general technophobia, and are often more reluctant to interact with machines than younger people

- The elderly are more likely to be motivated by, for example, genealogy programs than shoot 'em up style games

- Restrictions in mobility may make applications such as Email more attractive to the elderly and enable them to overcome physical mobility constraints

- Older adults tend to read documentation and screens more thoroughly than younger users, and to be more reluctant to take the plunge and start interacting with the system before studying the documentation

- Instructions and help should be supportive rather than challenging for older users

- Tutorial materials for older users should spell out differences compared to traditional activities, for example a word processing manual for older users needs to highlight the differences compared with typewriters, whilst a manual for a ten-year old need make no such contrast

- Tasks involving unusual manual dexterity and associated concepts, such as mouse use, scrolling, text block manipulation etc. will need careful explanation and practice for older users.

- Memorisation should be avoided for elderly users because of the decline in their short term memory

- It is often helpful to allow older adults to train in pairs

- Above all, it is important to avoid stereotypes of older users and to recognise that there will be major individual differences in abilities and performance for such users.

2.2.5 Users with special needs

This group is really many groups, since by definition they don't fit into specific categories. We can consider those with vision and hearing impairments, physical and mental special needs and possibly cultural special needs-some religious sects consider monitors as a form of television, and therefore the work of the devil.

Speech recognition and speech output devices allow those with visual impairments to use computers. IBM have just announced the plan to introduce a cheap PC based speech recognition system with a vocabulary of 25,000 words and training time of three hours. Such a system may eventually replace keyboards and mice for most users, not just the vision impaired. Speech output is already cheaply available, with software for speech synthesis often being included with sound cards. Such speech is rather unnatural, and rather boring to listen to for long periods because of the flat intonation used, but does open up the use of computers to wider groups in society.

Speech based input and output technologies offer the most scope for catering for those users with physical special needs, whilst standard VDUs and keyboards meet the needs of the hearing impaired.

2.2.6   Group workers (Computer Supported Co-operative Work or CSCW)

CSCW systems allow users in the same or different locations to communicate with co-workers at the same or different times.

CSCW environments may have a big impact on power relationships within work groups, and the study of such environments relies heavily on inputs from Sociology. The main focus is on the synchronous (same-time) forms of CSCW, since the asynchronous forms are little different from memo and postal based non-computer systems.

Typical groupworking conferencing systems use a shared whiteboard, visible to all participants, who can display and annotate data on the whiteboard for all to see. Data from applications can be used thanks to technologies such as OLE (Object Linking and Embedding) and DDE (Dynamic Data Exchange).

Question 2.1

Design a questionnaire that can be used to categorise different types of proposed computer system.

	Same time (synchronous)	**Different time (asynchronous)**
Same place	Meetings, tutorials etc. Participants all have portable computers linked to an electronic 'whiteboard' for sharing data with other participants.	Project scheduling and co-ordination. Computerised equivalent of internal memos.
Different places	Shared editors, on-line 'conferences' etc. The shared workspace allows contributions from participants. Lack of face-to-face contact and non-verbal cues can be overcome to some extent by the use of emoticons. There needs to be a method of controlling the dialogue and turn-taking.	Email, bulletin boards, Compuserve support forums. These are basically computerised extensions of the process of posting work from one part of an organisation to another, for continued processing.

A four-category classification for CSCW systems (based on Schneiderman 1992)

2.2.7 Factors that make users more likely to accept computerisation

Studies of managers and professionals have found that it is the perceived usefulness rather than perceived fun to use that is most influential in acceptance of computers, with usefulness about six times as important as fun in determining acceptance. User satisfaction was found to be less influential than either usefulness or fun. Perceived fun had more effect on user satisfaction than perceived usefulness, and may encourage users to explore new packages and features. Anxiety reduced levels of perceived fun, but anxiety could be reduced best by appropriate training. Reduced levels of anxiety lead to increased levels of computer use, so reducing anxiety through training is an important way of winning acceptance of computers. Perceived usefulness, perceived fun and levels of anxiety are all found to be more influential in affecting levels of computer usage than user satisfaction.

2.3 Claims analysis and stakeholders

In any organisation, different groups have different and often conflicting interests, and in order to assess the impact of new information systems we need to discover just who such Stakeholders are in the organisation and their motives and power relative to other groups, for example IT is often seen as a way that managers can increase their control over groups of workers. We need to be aware of such factors as well as analysing the task itself, since the ways in which tasks are performed can affect informal organisational structures and processes.

2.4 Human perception

Human perception is more than just seeing or hearing. It's an active process involving the interpretation of information in its context and the attribution of meaning. The following examples attempt to illustrate the active nature of the perceptual process: "The baby cried, the mother picked it up".

Most listeners to such a sentence interpret it as meaning that the mother of the baby that is crying picked it up to comfort it because it was crying. Yet there is nothing in the sentence to say that the baby and the mother are related, or that the picking-up was a consequence of the crying. Yet most listeners infer the same contextual information and interpret events in the same way. Our stock of such contextual knowledge means that we can usually successfully interpret most situations correctly and take appropriate actions. But when faced with new situations, we may not possess adequate contextual knowledge to correctly interpret situations. This is quite likely to be the case when introducing new information systems. Users don't necessarily have appropriate conceptual frameworks to help in the interpretation of interface information. The Swiss psychologist Piaget's concept of schema is useful to help us understand how users deal with new situation.

At first the user will apply existing ideas and methods to try to deal with the new situation, but if this is unsuccessful they will modify their existing schema, incorporating new knowledge and methods. For example, when children first move up from a tricycle to a two-wheel bike they initially use their schema for riding a tricycle. However, this will cause problems of balance which have to be accommodated by changing and adapting their schema. Similarly when confronted by a new piece of software, users will apply their old schema. But this may include product-specific knowledge such as keystroke shortcuts to perform certain actions, but if these differ in the new package compared with the old, users will have to adapt their schema. An analysis of users' existing schema will therefore be necessary to try to anticipate and design out interface problems.

2.4.1 Movement, change and perception

Our perceptual systems work to filter out continuous levels of data, concentrating instead on changes in data. This is how we are able to get used to steady levels of traffic noise, for example. This has implications for interface design, in that we notice changes in state, but if information remains on screen it will soon just become part of the perceptual background and will be ignored. We are more likely to notice movement than still images, hence the use of dials and bar charts in many software packages to keep us informed of the progress of operations such as installation routines. Conversely, users often fail to notice unchanging screen messages precisely because of the lack of motion.

2.4.2 3D effects and depth perception

We normally perceive depth as a result of the slightly different images seen in the right and left eyes. To demonstrate this, close one eye and hold a pencil at arms length. Line up the pencil with the edge of a door or window. Now close the eye and open the one that was previously closed. The pencil will no longer appear in line with the edge. We obviously can't use solid objects in two dimensional screens, but we can rely on our monocular (one-eyed) depth cues to create the illusion of depth in screen objects.

Monocular depth cues

Interposition: If part of one object obscures part of another, such as the two 'documents' on the Copy toolbar button in Word for Windows, we perceive the one that is obscured as being further away or behind the other.

Relative size: If we see two similar objects, but one is larger than the other, we perceive the larger one as closer than the other one.

Shadow: Shadows cast by an object provide cues as to relative position of objects. This is used to give GUI buttons a 3-D appearance.

Texture gradient: As the texture of a surface appears larger, the surface is perceived as closer.

Contrast and focus: Sharper objects appear to be closer than less distinct ones.

Motion parallax: If we look out of a moving train window, the names of the stations (which are very close) are difficult to read, whereas the scenery in the background appears to move much more slowly.

Question 2.2   Choose a GUI you are familiar with and list the icons that make use of monocular depth cues to create the impression that they are solid.

2.4.3 Colour perception

Since most of us (92% of males and over 99% of females) are able to perceive colour it is potentially very useful in interface design. Colour can be used to make different parts of the screen stand out, for example the active window in Microsoft Windows has its menu bar coloured blue, and this draws our attention to the active window. Similarly, colour can be used to highlight particular parts of the display, for example areas of the screen that require user input. When using colour we need to remember that not all colours can be successfully combined. Generally, bright foreground colours should be used on a dark or dim background, hence the popularity of white text on a dark blue background in word processors such as WordStar and WordPerfect for DOS.

Question 2.3

If you have access to Microsoft Windows, experiment with changing the default colours for foreground and background. Make a note of any combinations that are particularly difficult.

2.5 Semiotics and icons

Semiotics is the science of signs. It is concerned with how we attribute meaning to objects in terms of some existing code, for example the UK Highway code enables motorists to correctly attribute meaning to road signs by reference to the code, and some of these conventional signs also work as icons in computer interfaces, such as the Windows Stop! sign or the Compuserve green traffic light for Go!. But other signs and symbols have more ambiguous meanings when we try to use them in the computing context, for example the piggy bank icon for File Save of Microsoft Excel, later abandoned for a 3.5″ floppy disk symbol.

Icon Design

General Icon Specifications

Icon sizes
- Standard: VGA, EGA, CGA, 8514 (Super VGA) = 32x32 pixels.
- Small: VGA, EGA, CGA, 8514 (Super VGA) = 16x16 pixels.

Color

- 16-color icons should use Windows 16-color palette.
- Use primarily the lighter colors from the color palettes.
- Use color appropriately and with restraint.

Image style

- When possible, base icons on real-world objects.
- Make icons illustrative but with only necessary detail.
- Make black outlined images.

3-D objects

- When possible, depict icons as three-dimensional objects.
- If the object is flat (e.g., paper) put a shadow on the right and bottom edges.

Microsoft Visual Basic's Icon design guide

Answer 2.2	*Answers include the bold, italic and underline 'buttons' in Word for Windows and many others.*
Answer 2.3	*Choices such as white foreground and yellow background will make text difficult to read.*

Modern Graphical User Interfaces such as Windows, the Macintosh interface and Motif make extensive use of icons to represent common actions. However the extent to which icons make an interface more usable depends on the extent to which users are familiar with the coding system used for the icons. As GUIs become increasingly popular, conventions will become established for representing common actions (such as the file open icon in WordPerfect and Word for Windows) to novice users, thereby increasing the ease of learning of new software that makes use of such conventions.

Question 2.4

Try to identify the following icons. How important is context for determining the meaning of icons?

Question 2.5

Choose a GUI you are familiar with. List it's default icons, categorising them into those that use existing non-computing conventions, such as the green traffic light for Go in Compuserve, and those that don't.

2.5.1 Emoticons

Emoticons are ways of expressing emotions such as happy, sad, winking, frowning etc. on text-only terminals and PCs. They are often used on the Internet. Some examples of icons for text-based systems include the following. Tilt your head to the left and you will see the effect:

:-)	happy
:-(	sad
;-)	wink
:-D	said with a smile
:-o	shout
:~i	smoking
<:-)	dumb question
@>—->—	a rose

2.6 Memory

As we discussed above, our perception tends to focus on changes in our environment rather than on stable information. Such selective attention means that much of what appears in an interface is likely to be ignored by the user, so it is vital to ensure that important information is presented in ways that will catch our attention (and that unnecessary information is not displayed on the screen).

2.6.1 Short-term memory

STM can be thought of rather like a scratchpad or an area of RAM in a computer, providing a temporary store for information that is not required to be stored in long-term memory. For example, we don't need to commit to Long-term memory (LTM) the stages we go through in performing a calculation. Humans can only remember approximately seven items of new information, plus or minus two. So a system that requires users to remember more than seven items will pose great difficulty for most users.

2.6.2 Long-term memory

LTM is concerned with the retrieval of information rather like retrieving information from a database. Just as most database retrieval problems stem from knowing where to find the information, so human LTM retrieval problems are usually due to a failure to retrieve information at the time required rather than actually forgetting the information.

2.6.2.1 Chunking

Chunking is the organisation of data into meaningful units, in order to improve our ability to remember. For example, the sequence 8396501751 is very difficult for humans to remember. Yet the sequence 0171 834 3467 is much easier to remember since we recognise it as a telephone number for central London, and we chunk telephone numbers into exchange codes and individual telephone numbers. Such chunking allows us to break the 7+–2 limit for STM.

Question 2.6   List some other ways in which we chunk information.

Answer 2.4	*These are all Windows icons, from the main and accessories program groups.*
Answer 2.5	*You can divide icons into three kinds, those like the Compuserve traffic light that use non-computing specific codes, those that use well-accepted computing-specific codes such as floppy disk and scissors icons, and those that are much more obscure such as the 'Insert Frame' button on the Word for Windows toolbar.*
Answer 2.6	*Car number plates (especially in countries like France and Italy, which use area codes).*

2.7 Human reasoning

Software manual writers nearly all seem to assume that if you set down in the correct order a step-by-step description of how to perform tasks this is all that is necessary for users to learn how to use the package. Such approaches never seem to work however, because human reasoning and actions are not quite as logical as we sometimes think.

2.7.1 Deductive reasoning

This is the scientific kind of reasoning where we state premises such as:

> *John is Mary's brother Brothers and sisters are not allowed to marry.*

We then deduce logically necessary conclusions from these premises:

> *John and Mary are not allowed to marry.*

The programming language Prolog (short for Programming in Logic) is based on such deductive reasoning. But humans rarely use deductive reasoning, instead relying on their taken-for-granted knowledge about the world based on their own experiences. Logically we may know that a Rover car is manufactured in Japan, by a German-owned company, and that a Nissan is manufactured in Britain, but most motorists would, if asked, reply that the Rover was a British car, and the Nissan a Japanese one. When human experience conflicts with logical deduction, it is logic that is usually abandoned. The recognition that people don't always think logically has important implications for interface design, and helps explain why so much software isn't used in the ways predicted by software designers. It also means that it is necessary to actually test software interfaces to see what people actually do with them, rather than trying to deduce what actions users will perform.

Question 2.7	Imagine that in front of you are two boxes labelled black and white respectively. There are 10 white shapes in the white box and 10 black shapes in the black box. The only shapes are triangles and circles. How can you prove the following proposition true in as few steps as possible: If they are triangles, then they are black.

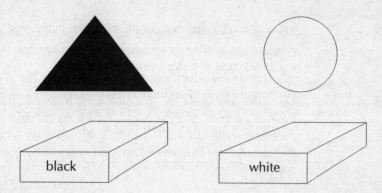

2.7.2 Inductive reasoning

This is where we generalise from past experience. If hitting a television that isn't working properly has often appeared to fix the television, we may infer that hitting other electrical goods that aren't working properly will fix them. Much human reasoning is based on induction-if something worked in a seemingly similar situation before, we will use it again. Many novice users of software will try commands from other packages when they get stuck. Of course, this is a totally unreliable way to reason about things and is often quite incorrect, but is widely used by humans. Because we rely so much on induction, it is as well to standardise ways to perform common actions in software, so that problem-solving strategies based on induction are likely to work (and unfortunately to contribute to the idea that induction is a good approach to reasoning). Examples include the way that much software has standard-ised on the use of the F1 key to call up help, or the ESC key to take the user back to the previous screen.

Question 2.8   Think of some examples of inductive reasoning among computer users

2.7.3 Abductive reasoning

This is where we reason from a fact to an explanation, for example, if we find that when using a mouse the text on our display seems to scroll past much too fast, we may reason that it is the action of using the mouse itself, rather than our inexpert use of it, that makes the text move too fast. Abduction involves confusing the correlation between two things with evidence that one event caused the other, and is very common in humans.

2.7.4 Conclusions on reasoning

Of the three types of reasoning above, inductive and abductive are by far the most common. Yet both are flawed and incomplete. This has important implications for interface designers.

Question 2.9   You have just returned from holiday in August to find that you left your freezer switched off. Luckily it was empty at the time. You want to re-stock it and need to get it down to it's normal temperature of -3 degrees C as quickly as possible. Should you set the thermostat control to:

1.   the minimum temperature possible

Answer 2.7

Most people attempting the task ask for black shapes at first. To prove the proposition you need to establish that there are no white triangles. The contents of the black box are irrelevant.

Answer 2.8

You often see users trying commands from other software when they aren't sure how to perform an operation. Switching off and re-starting the computer is quite commonplace, but for systems using windows leads to the creation of many temporary files that would normally be deleted, eventually filling all available disk space.

2. −3C exactly.

3. the maximum setting.

Clearly such settings are examples of badly designed interfaces. Incidentally, your answer to the question may have been based on the fact that your own freezer has a fast freeze setting, a good example of how our own experience interferes with our ability to reason logically from premises to conclusions.

2.8 Metaphors and conceptual models

A metaphor is just a way of explaining something new by focusing on its similarities with a familiar object. For example, word processors are typically explained by comparing them with typewriters. In interface design much use has been made of desktop metaphors where the screen contains icons for familiar office objects as files, waste bins, clocks and calendars etc. However, as well as similarities between new and familiar objects, there are also differences, and if the metaphor is taken too far this can cause difficulties. For example, many users new to word processors make the mistake of treating the Caps Lock key just as they would on a typewriter, but this doesn't work when they want to type symbols such as : and %. The desktop metaphors prevalent on computers today, such as Windows and Macintosh, owe their origins to the Xerox Star interface developed in the late 1970s. Metaphors make it easy to learn about unfamiliar objects, but need to be carefully designed since interfaces often need to combine metaphors from more than one area, and to represent actions that are not possible (such as saving, cutting and pasting on typewriters) on the familiar object. However, it seems that people don't have too much trouble building up composite metaphors such as the Windows interface with its combination of familiar objects with the less familiar such as the cut and paste metaphors borrowed from newspaper and magazine production. But it is important that users' actions don't result in undesirable consequences such as the loss or deletion of work since this may make them reluctant to experiment and increase their knowledge of the software.

Question 2.10

Think of some more metaphors used in computing.

2.8.1 Conceptual models

Conceptual models are the mental images that humans form in order to understand something. Human behaviour occurs against a background of such conceptual models, and they form guidelines for action even if they are completely inappropriate or just plain wrong. For example when the Chinese peasantry rose up to join the Chinese Communist party in overthrowing their rulers in 1949 many did so as a result of conceptual models based on the teachings of Confucius that taught that the uprising was a sign from the gods that the 'mandate from heaven' to rule had passed from the old regime to the Communist party. It doesn't actually matter whether a particular conceptual model is correct or not, people who hold such a model will still behave as though it were true.

In interface design, we also need to take account of conceptual models. Most software development involves the software developer constructing a conceptual model of the desired system, based on systems analysis and design methods. The developer's model is then implemented as the software package. If the interface and supporting material is well implemented, the user's conceptual model should correspond more or less exactly to the developer's conceptual model. However, in practice this is rarely the case. The result of such a lack of correspondence or mismatch is an interface and system that is poorly understood by the user and therefore difficult for them to use efficiently. This mismatch is also known as the 'Gulf of execution' of a system. Of course it can also happen that the developer has only a partial grasp of the end users' requirements and designs a system that only meets some of the users' requirements. Good design involves the designer taking responsibility for bridging the gulf, so that as far as possible the designer's and user's conceptual models match each other. Practical ways to achieve this are discussed in Chapter 6.

2.8.2 Discovering user's conceptual models

An important task for the developer is to find out as much as possible about the user's conceptual models. Participative approaches to systems analysis and design emphasise the importance of such an approach. Soft Systems Methodology and Multiview are two examples of Participative analysis and design. These are covered in more depth in Chapter 5.

2.9 Social aspects of human-computer interaction

The use of computers occurs within social settings and contexts, notably the work setting. But all too often the socially-situated nature of computer use has been ignored in favour of attempts to model individual cognitive processes such as memory and reasoning. However, recognition that context of use affects user behaviour has shifted the focus of attention away from the individual and individual psychological processes to the social and sociological processes. Contextual inquiry involves users and evaluators identifying issues in the natural work setting, using discussions and interviews to try and reveal the interpretations users place on their interface behaviour. It doesn't matter whether or not a group of users has an 'incorrect' view of the purpose and result of a particular action, since what guides their behaviour is their understanding of what is happening (just like the Chinese peasants in 1949, when their Confucian religion lead many to believe that 'the mandate from heaven' had passed from China's KMT ruling party to the Chinese Communist party, with the result that they supported the Chinese revolution). For example, observation of casual users of Excel 4 often reveals that after having produced a chart using the 'chart wizard', users expect to be able to step back through the stages to edit the chart, since this facility is available to them during the chart creation stage. But no such facility is available, leading to frustration for users. Such a situation is an example of a mismatch between designer and user views of the system.

Answer 2.9

You should set it to –3C exactly. Many people incorrectly assume that the correct answer is number 1. But setting the thermostat to a lower temperature doesn't affect the speed of cooling. The thermostat is simply an on/off switch activated when the pre-set temperature is reached. Many refrigerators and freezers have dials marked maximum and minimum, but whilst this would cause no problem on an oven, it does on a fridge, since the maximum setting could either mean the coldest setting, or the warmest!

Answer 2.10

We often explain databases as electronic filing cabinets, or spread sheets as electronic analysis paper etc.

Question 2.11

Choose a package you are familiar with and observe some novice or occasional users using the package. Record details of any examples of conceptual model mismatches that occur.

Ethnography uses techniques with their origins in Sociology and anthropology which require the systems analyst to set aside all their preconceptions about the users and to attempt to record as much information as possible about behaviour in the work context, asking questions even when the answers seem obvious. Video recording is often used, and multiple views of the same situation collected from different users in the same workplace, which can then be compared and discussed. User conceptual models can then be developed for the end-user tasks. Speech Act theory is based on the philosophy of language and assumes that when we make an 'utterance' (when we say something) in a conversation we are performing an action, and that the listener then has to choose whether to accept the implied conditions, reject them, try to negotiate the conditions, or seek a withdrawal of the speaker's request. In face-to-face communications we use a range of non-verbal cues such as facial expression, gesture, direction of gaze etc. all of which help us to understand the real meaning of the communication. We can literally say one thing verbally, but say the opposite with our gestures, expressions etc. As groupworking becomes more important, there is greater scope for misunderstandings since with present technologies many of these non-verbal cues are absent. In response to this, systems have been designed that spell-out explicitly the options (accept, reject, re negotiate or seek withdrawal) available and displays them on a menu for the listener to choose. It is claimed that such speech act systems avoid the likelihood of misunderstandings in communication since explicit commitments have to be made. However, there is little evidence to support these claims, and advances in full-motion video conferencing and CSCW systems such as IBM's People to People are likely to reduce the need for such systems in future. As more systems are designed for co-operative work environments, or for open communications networks, Sociological techniques are likely to become increasingly important.

2.10 Organisational factors in human-computer interaction

Organisations differ in their culture or way of doing things, in their aims and purposes, in the way in which work and workers are organised and the way in which technologies, including IT, are used. Each of these will affect the design of computer systems and their acceptance by workers in the organisation. For example, in organisations where IT has caused large-scale job loss and weakened the power of trade unions, such as newspaper publishing, we would expect greater suspicion of new systems than in organisations where IT had enriched and expanded the numbers of jobs.

2.10.1 The importance of context of use

It is all very well to design an interface for particular tasks and users, but we also need to take account of the context of use. In an organisation where IT has lead to job losses, de-skilling and greater control by managers, we would expect workers to be much more reluctant to embrace new systems than in an organisation where IT had the opposite effects. Similarly, systems designed for entertainment and home users need to take account of differences compared with the work environment (and vice versa-features that improve the interface of a computer game wouldn't necessarily work in a business application).

Measuring context

The National Physical Laboratory breaks context of use down into the following categories:

- Equipment: application area and functions, hardware and software. Includes a basic description of the product and its intended use.

- Users: skills, knowledge and personal attributes e.g. age, gender, attitude and motivation, intellectual abilities, product and task experience, level of experience.

- Task: goals, frequency, duration, physical and mental demands, risks as a result of errors

- Environment: working conditions, organisational attitudes and culture, health and safety factors, job design, payment systems etc.

NPL use a detailed questionnaire to identify all relevant factors under each of the above headings and to assess whether or not they are likely to affect the usability of the particular product or system being tested, for example a system to be used by experienced programmers would obviously be less likely to be affected by factors such as experience of computer systems, general level of education etc. as one aimed at end-users.

2.10.2 User motivations

Systems analysts need to identify the different Stakeholders (interest groups) in a work environment and their concerns, issues and values. To understand the organisational context of an Information System we need to investigate system Stakeholders, their motivations, organisational rituals (such as meetings, which are often about displays of power) and symbols (e.g. many managers have much more powerful computers than they need, as a mark of their status). We also need to acknowledge that many functions are covert (hidden) and that there will often be conflicts between different Stakeholders in the organisation. For example, in some situations it is even possible that decisions to purchase a particular system could be taken by someone who has informal links with the system's supplier. Such situations may border on the criminal, but undoubtedly do occur from time to time.

Answer 2.11   *Typical examples might include users trying to undo several actions, rather than the one most recent action usually supported, or trying to edit documents in read-only mode*

Question 2.12   Analyse the main Stakeholders and their motivations in an organisation you are familiar with.

Review questions

1. Describe the main types of computer users and their particular requirements.

2. How can designers describe and analyse the tasks that different groups of users of a system perform?

3. What role can semiotics play in the design of the human computer interface?

4. Do humans always think logically? What are the implications of your answer for interface designers?

5. How does an understanding of users' conceptual models help in the design of the interface?

6. Why do designers need to take account of the context of use of a system?

Test questions

1. What role can traditional systems analysis techniques such as data flow diagrams, entity relationship diagrams and JSP diagrams play in interface design?

2. What psychological and social factors do system designers need to take into account when designing systems?

3. How can designers analyse and represent user tasks and user conceptual models?

3 Technology

3.1 Introduction

This chapter looks at the hardware and software side of human-computer interaction. It considers input and output devices, styles of human-computer interaction, multimedia interaction, windows-based systems, and training and support materials to help users learn, use and troubleshoot when using systems.

- Keyboards
- Health and safety issues and keyboards: WRULDS and RSI
- Non-keyboard input
- Output devices
- Interaction styles
- Training materials
- Help and reference information
- On-line forums on Compuserve, the Internet etc.

3.2 Input devices

These are ways of getting data into machine readable form, either directly or indirectly. Of course if data is already in computer readable form, for example as a file on a disk or tape, it can be transferred to other computers with appropriate hardware and software, although such transfers can be quite tricky to set up and use reliably. Such transfers are the subject matter of computer communications, and warrant an entire book in themselves.

3.2.1 Transferring data from other computers

If the computers are in the same location, the easiest way to transfer the data is via a floppy disk assuming the systems hardware and software are compatible with each other. Failing this, two computers can often be connected and data transferred using a serial link and appropriate software such as the Laplink program, or MS-DOS Interlink. Where computers are on different sites, data may be transferred via the telephone network using modems and communications software.

3.2.2 Keyboards

There are several different types of keyboard available for computers.

Qwerty

The QWERTY keyboard was actually designed to slow typists down last century since more efficient layouts and higher typing speeds actually caused the mechanical arms on which the letters were set to jam. Since such limitations do not apply to computer keyboards, it seems logical to try to design more efficient layouts to increase potential keyboarding rates. However, as we shall see, things aren't quite that simple. Note that the AZERTY keyboard is a variant of the QWERTY keyboard used in France and other French-speaking countries. There is no letter w in French, other than in imported words such as week-end, whisky, w.c. etc. The letter q is used much more frequently than in English, however. Other variations include the £ sign on UK keyboards, but not on US ones.

Alphabetic

The alphabetic keyboard simply arranges letters in alphabetical order, so that inexperienced users won't have to search the keyboard for the letter they want. However, such an approach fails to take account of the fact that we use some letters, such as e and s, much more frequently than others, such as x and z. Alphabetic keyboards offer no speed advantages to touch typists anyway.

Dvorak

The Dvorak keyboard, designed in the 1930s, takes account of the frequency of use of letters and the workload distribution between the two hands. On a Dvorak keyboard, the five vowels together with the most frequently used consonants are placed on the middle row of keys, with lesser used keys placed on the top and bottom rows. Typists using the Dvorak keyboard typically make fewer errors than with a QWERTY keyboard, and are up to 10% faster. However, the need to retrain millions of typists and replace millions of keyboards has limited the success of the Dvorak keyboard.

Other types of keyboard

Left-handed keyboards. These are similar to a Qwerty keyboard except that the cursor movement, Home and End keys are moved from the right to the left hand side, on the principal that left-handed users will prefer to use their left hand more than their right. However, there seems little evidence to bear this out in practice, with left handed users of such keyboards still tending to automatically look to the right for the transposed keys.

Small keyboards

Standard keyboards are approximately 50cm by 20 cm (20" by 8"). Laptop and sub-notebook computers typically use smaller keyboards of necessity, since they need to be small for portability, and typically measure around 30cm by 22cm (12" by 9" or A4 size). The typical size of keyboard on such portables is around 30cm by 10cm, and although they usually have fewer than the 101/102 key norm found on desktops, users usually report that such small keyboards are harder to use than full-size ones. So-called pocket computers such as the Psion series 3 and Atari Portfolio have to make even greater compromises with keyboards and are even less satisfactory for normal keyboarding tasks.

Numeric keypads

Tasks requiring high volumes of numerical data input benefit from a numeric keyboard. The standard PC-AT 101/102 keyboard comes with a numeric keypad section on the right hand side, and is particularly useful for spreadsheet data entry. The lack of space for numeric keypads is one of the design compromises typically found on notebook and laptop computers, and it is usually possible to purchase add-on numeric keypads for them where required.

Chord keyboards e.g. Microwriter

In these there are only a few keys which are used in different combinations to form each letter, for example on an early design of chord keyboard with five keys, the letter a was produced by pressing key 5, b by pressing key 4, c by pressing 4 and 5 together, d by pressing 3, e by pressing 3 and 5 etc.

Such keyboards are very compact, and suitable for one-handed operation (although in practice many inexperienced typists only use one hand, or two fingers, with normal keyboards). They take only a few hours to learn and are capable of quite high speeds, but are tiring to use compared to normal keyboards.

Other aspects of keyboard design

Users of different keyboards soon realise that some keyboards are pleasanter to use than others, regardless of the actual layout of the keys. Each key is in fact a switch which, when depressed, makes a circuit and sends a signal to the computer. The 'feel' of a keyboard is determined by the type of keys used and the amount of travel. Some keyboards use individual sprung switches which make a positive click as the key is depressed, while others make do with a thin rubber or plastic membrane. The latter are usually found to be less satisfactory than those which make an audible click, since the click is important auditory feedback that tells the user that the key has successfully been depressed, and the importance of this should not be underestimated.

The amount of keyboards travel is also important, since laptop keyboard designs often reduce the travel in order to reduce the space required, thereby allowing the laptop to be thinner than would otherwise be the case. Such reduced-travel keys can appear to lack feedback to users, although with practice one becomes used to the limited travel.

Sealed-membrane keyboards

These are often found on the front panels of older dot-matrix printers, usually with the membrane ruptured! Such keyboards are supposed to be touch-sensitive, and are sealed to prevent dirt etc. entering the mechanism. However, they often provide insufficient feedback (hence users push them harder and more times than are necessary, so you often find the membrane torn – see if you can find any such devices and look to see what state the membranes are in). However, in particularly hostile environments, such as on the shop floor or out of doors, their sealed design can make them essential.

Special keys

Function keys: Keyboards typically provide 12 function keys used for keyboard shortcuts, either alone or in combination with other keys such as the SHIFT, ALT and CTRL keys 48 shortcuts can be provided. Much software also allows user customisation of the function key assignments. It is important to make novice users aware of the function keys and their use.

Cursor movement keys

These are the up, down, left and right arrow keys, and usually also the PgDn, PgUp, Home and End keys. Common user problems with these are lack of awareness of the function of the PgUp and PgDn, Home and End keys, and users often try to move the cursor beyond the end of their file with the down key, and confusion concerning the operation of the backspace, Del and Ins keys.

Conclusions on keyboards

Evidence suggests that for most text entry tasks standard Qwerty keyboards with full-travel 'click' keys are the preferred option. Since keyboards represent such a small proportion of the price of a PC (typically 2-5%) yet are the most common input device, it is worth selecting keyboards carefully with end-user feedback.

Keyboards which don't provide feedback have the greatest effect on touch typists' performance, even after allowing practice with such keyboards they typically reduce speed by 20% and double error rates, with not surprisingly lower levels of user satisfaction being reported for such non-feedback keyboards.

Question 3.1

Construct a chart listing all of the different types of keyboards mentioned above. List their advantages and disadvantages and special areas of application for each.

Health and Safety issues and keyboards: WRULDS and RSI

During the 1980s increasing concern has been raised over work-related upper limb disorders (WRULDS) affecting fingers, hands and arms, the best-known of which is repetitive strain injury (RSI). There have now been several well-documented court cases where employees have successfully won damages in the courts for injuries caused by keyboarding, and it is now widely accepted that high keyboard usage cause such WRULDS. In the light of the health and safety concerns, we are likely to see an end to the search for faster keyboard layouts, since speed of keying is acknowledged as one of the causes of WRULDS. However, more effort is being channelled into the design of keyboards with better ergonomics: in late 1994 Microsoft introduced their own ergonomic 'Natural' keyboard with the keys set at more natural angles and a wrist rest incorporated at the front of the keyboard.

3.2.3 Non-keyboard input

There are a range of non-keyboard input devices that largely automate data capture to such an extent that there are few, if any interface considerations to take into account. However, the suitability of such devices is still something which designers need to rake into account when designing systems, since they are not always suitable for all types of user in all environments, and users still need training in their accurate and effective use.

Optical Mark Readers (OMR)

Most of us have probably come across OMR at some time. OMR documents are typically completed by users marking a box with a pencil, usually by drawing a line in the relevant box. They are much used in multiple-choice tests, and are used by some educational exam boards for recording the marks awarded to candidates. The completed OMR documents are machine-read, the OM reader detecting the presence of the pencil mark and its position and converting this to the appropriate entry to a blank field in a database.

Answer to 3.1

	QWERTY	DVORAK	Sealed-membrane	Alphabetic	Left-handed	Small	Chord
Advantages	Best for general use	Fast	Dirt etc. resistant	Good for novices	Cursor etc. keys on left	Compact	Compact
Disadvantages	Limits speed	Experienced users need retraining	Slow, poor feedback	Slows down experienced users	Experienced users look for them on the right	Slower, less feedback	Tiring to use

OMR requires no special equipment or training for end users, and allows the fast input of large quantities of data, together with validation and error checking. However, it is only suitable for certain types of input such as numeric data, multiple-choice questions or closed questionnaire responses.

Optical Character Readers (OCR)

Optical character recognition is a familiar technology. Look at utility bills such as gas, electricity or telephone bills and you will often find the use of an OCR font which is both human and machine readable at the bottom of the bill. Such systems have been around since the 1970s and are reliable for high volumes of data. The main disadvantage is that they require special printing of the precise font. Advances in the reliability of OCR software and scanners, together with greater use of bar-coding, may reduce the requirement for special fonts and printing. A major advantage of OCR over bar-coding is that the information is human-readable.

Bar Code Readers

The familiar supermarket bar-codes are now a reliable technology, although when first used on a large scale in supermarkets in the mid-1980s they were not well received by customers as the system was so unreliable, with customers finding that the price displayed alongside the goods bore no relationship to the price charged at the till, to the extent that the supermarket concerned started to lose market share to rivals who had not adopted the technology. Indeed there were several reports of shops using the systems being prosecuted by trading standards officers for displaying misleading price information. The author has personal experience of mis-matches between displayed prices and those encoded and charged by several shops, usually in favour of the shops! However, advances in accuracy of recognition have reduced the scale of the problem. Environments where the codes can become smudged, such as outdoor use in a garden centre, require special consideration, such as the manufacturer pre-printing standard bar codes on, for example, water-resistant plastic tags attached at the factory, or pre-printed steel cans.

Magnetic Card Readers

Credit and debit cards, electronic 'keys' and similar devices rely on the encoding of data on a short strip of magnetic tape on the back of the card. Data is encoded according to ANSI or ISO standards, on up to three tracks. Total capacity on the three tracks is 226 characters. More recently 'smartcards' have been developed, initially in France, which incorporate a ROM or PROM chip allowing much greater data capacity. Card readers can be purchased for connection to PCs, and such devices have recently been implicated in the so-called 'phantom' cashcard withdrawals from bank ATM machines.

Magnetic Ink Character Recognition (MICR)

This is the use of magnetically readable characters, and its best known implementation in the UK is in cheque clearing. The highly stylised and just about human-readable numbers at the bottom of cheques are MICR characters for the cheque number, branch sort code and account number. The only data that needs to be entered manually is the amount of the cheque, the other details being read by the MICR reader. MICR looks similar to OCR, although it uses quite different magnetic rather than optical technology.

Scanners

The technology behind OCR and bar-codes is that of scanning. A scanner uses a charge-coupled device (CCD) to detect the presence or absence of marks. The technology is also used in fax machines. Once a document has been scanned, a bitmap image of it is produced, in a format similar to the graphics file formats used by painting packages such as MacDraw and Windows Paintbrush. These resulting bitmaps can then be stored, displayed and transmitted by modem or other means. This is the basis of fax transmission. However, the bitmaps can also be read by optical character recognition software, which will attempt to turn the bitmap into text.

Different OCR software packages differ in their ability to read particular typefaces. Most can read standard typefaces such as Courier, Times, Helvetica etc. in 10–12 point, but many have problems with more stylised fonts, such as italic and gothic fonts, and with very large or small font sizes. Also, the accuracy and speed of the scanning will affect the ability to read text, since letters can become stretched and distorted during scanning. This is a particular problem with hand-held scanners. Nevertheless, even cheap OCR software can typically reach 98% accuracy at recognition speeds faster than those of even the fastest typists. A flat-bed scanner, good OCR software and a spell checker allows good quality OCR input.

Flat-bed scanners

See above. These allow accurate scanning of items, but are usually only suitable for single sheets rather than books. They produce much better results than hand-held devices, since the item is held firmly in place and the speed of the scan is controlled precisely.

Hand-held scanners

These are more flexible than flat-bed devices, but only allow smaller scans, typically a maximum of 4" wide, and the image produced is usually poorer since the scanner is subject to shakes and wobbles by the operator and variations in scanning speed. The most successful hand-held scanners at present are probably the hand-held bar-code readers used in many retail outlets.

Fax

Not a direct input device, but fax machines are in effect scanners, and can be converted into flat-bed scanners to provide input.

Question 3.2   Distinguish between OCR, OMR and MICR input devices. Give examples of suitable applications for each. Which are the most user-friendly for casual users?

Touch screens

Touch screens either use a transparent plastic membrane which senses where the screen has been touched, or they use infra-red light beams which are shone across the screen vertically and horizontally. On touching the screen, the light beams are broken and the appropriate action is initiated.

Touch screens are intuitive to use, being suitable for simple menu selection systems such as a screen for obtaining local tourist information in a tourist information centre. However, they don't allow fine control and manipulation. They are tiring to use because the hand needs to be held at an unnatural angle, and the screens suffer from dirt. They are suited to only limited operations such as selecting items from a menu. They also don't offer much feedback to the user.

British Telecom has developed a prototype home teleshopping system using touch screen technology to select from a selection of icons for telephones, answering machines, BT services etc.

Joysticks

Joysticks are widely used in games and in flight simulators. They work in similar ways to mice for moving a cursor across the screen, but don't usually allow rapid cursor movement across the screen.

Mice

The mouse can be used both for cursor movement and for selecting items from menus, selecting and dragging icons etc. Mice allow accurate positioning and rapid cursor movement, as well as giving the impression of direct manipulation of desktop objects. However, the user needs room on his or her desktop to move the mouse around. Some manufacturers produce left-handed and children's' mice, with for example, the moulding being higher on one side than the other in the case of left-handed mice, and smaller with whiskers and a tail in the case of mice for children.

Footmouse

As its name suggests, this is a mouse-like device operated by the foot. Tilting the footmouse left or right or up or down moves the cursor in the appropriate direction. Just as we use our feet when driving a car, there is no reason why we shouldn't when using a computer, and footmice leave both hands free for other tasks (or allow those with only one hand to enjoys the benefits of using a mouse).

Question 3.3

How easy to use do you think a footmouse would be? Give reasons for your answer.

Trackball

This is really just an upside-down mouse, with the advantage that you don't need room on the desk surface to move it around.

Light pen

These operate in similar ways to mice and trackballs, but the user draws directly on the screen with the light pen. They have the advantage of directness and intuitiveness, but are tiring to use because of the need to hold them to the screen

Answer 3.2

The main use of MICR is in banking. Many customer bills from large organisations use OCR. OMR can be used for input by members of the public with no special equipment, whereas MICR and OCR require special equipment and are therefore less easy to use, although all produce human-readable characters compared with bar-codes.

Answer 3.3

Using a footmouse is probably little different from using the pedals on a car, or the treadle on old-fashioned sewing machines, and is surprisingly intuitive.

Graphics or digitizing tablet

The user moves a stylus or puck around on a small flat tablet on the work surface. This causes corresponding movement of the cursor on the screen, in much the same way as a mouse. Graphics tablets are good for drawing, and are more intuitive to use than mice. However, they require more desk space than mice. Large floor-standing digitizing tablets are also available, and work in the same way.

Still digital camera e.g. Canon Ion

These are like ordinary cameras, but store still images directly to a minidisk rather than to film. The image file can then be used just like any other graphics image file. A

popular application is to use them to replace photographs on identity cards. Instead, the person stands in front of the camera which captures a digitised image which is then used to produce the membership or identity card straight away, typically in around 30 seconds. It is also possible to achieve a similar result indirectly using an ordinary 35mm camera but having the film processed using the Kodak photo-CD process which stores the images digitally on CD. The images can then be used with a CD-ROM drive.

Moving video

Video cameras can be used to capture images which can then be converted to computer-readable form with suitable hardware and software. However, moving video images currently lack resolution and quality on today's PCs. Developments in video compression techniques and graphics accelerator cards are likely to make moving video on CD-ROM a realistic possibility very shortly, even on 80386 based computers with appropriate video accelerators.

Full motion video is defined as 15-30 frames per second, with television typically using between 25-30 fps. Below 15 fps the animation is too jerky to be perceived as full motion.

Full motion video may be full-screen, or part-screen, typically quarter-screen, with a proportionate reduction in memory and processing requirements.

A CD-ROM could contain all of the following data:

- 20 min of full-screen 30 fps full-motion video

- 80 min of quarter screen 15 fps full motion video

- 10 hours of AM radio quality audio (for speech)

- 2,000 still images

- 5 Megabytes of text and graphics

Videophone

Moving video can also be used to allow deaf users to communicate using sign language. Olivetti has recently launched its PCC 2.0 Videophone system for sign language users, comprising a PC with a telephone interface board, a handset and a miniature video camera that sits on top of the PC's monitor. Picture quality is good enough to allow communication using sign language, with the monitor displaying an image of the caller at the end of the line. The system requires an ISDN line rather than an ordinary line. Deaf users who are unable to sign can 'chat' using the keyboard. At present the PCC 2.0 upgrade kit costs around £3,500 plus the cost of a PC and ISDN line, but those in the UK with disabilities can apply to the Department of Employment Access to Work fund for financial assistance of up to £21,000 over a five year period for equipment to enable them to start or keep a job.

Videoconferencing systems

Videoconferencing systems typically allow several users to share a screen 'whiteboard' or notebook which they can all access, and to see moving video images of other conference participants on their screen simultaneously. They are 'groupware' or CSCW (Computer Supported Co-operative Work) systems that allow virtual meetings to take place over a LAN or over high-bandwidth telephone lines such as ISDN lines. Examples include IBM's Person to Person (P2P) and Intel's Proshare systems. Typically a miniature video camera with fixed-focus lens is mounted on top of the VDU, and video compression and ISDN cards allow video and voice communication over ISDN lines. On-screen keypads allow dialling of participant's phone numbers. The on-screen shared notebook or whiteboard typically has highlighting tools to simulate fluorescent marker pens, and line, box and circle drawing tools and pointers. Object linking allows documents to be loaded into the system and shared editing to take place. The screen also typically has a private work area for notes etc. that isn't visible to other users.

Such videoconferencing systems typically cost around £3000 per terminal (including pentium-based PC) plus the cost of a leased line, but document sharing only versions such as IBM's P2P software to allow up to eight users to share documents over a LAN is bundled free with its new OS/2 Warp operating system software.

This latest generation of videoconferencing systems represents an exciting attempt to overcome some of the problems associated with email-based groupware systems identified in Chapter 3 and discussed further inChapter 5.

Question 3.4   Distinguish between video phones, video conferencing and CSCW systems.

Dataglove

The Dataglove allows direct manipulation of objects in 'virtual worlds' such as simulated surgery on an ill virtual patient. The glove contains pressure and movement sensors connected to a display terminal or virtual reality headset. They allow 3-D manipulation of images and objects.

Penpad Computers e.g. Apple Newton, Amstrad Penpad

These are hand-held handwriting recognition devices that allow input using a pen to write letters and numbers on the screen. Such devices are considerably slower for text input than a keyboard. They also have to be trained to recognise the user's handwriting, making them unsuitable where several users share machines.

Answer 3.4

Videophones are simply sound and image communication devices, CSCW systems cover all groupworking systems, from Email to shared whiteboard and videoconferencing systems. Email and videophone systems don't allow document sharing.

Head movement headset

Used for severely disabled. The headset transmits slight head movements to allow selection of items from menus, key presses etc.

Speech recognition

Speech recognition systems fall broadly into two groups: control systems which allow users to speak commands such as 'save file', 'delete this line', 'go back two pages' etc., and dictation systems, which allow recognition and processing of normal every day continuous speech.

Control systems have long been possible, since only a limited range of commands need to be recognised. They can be used in situations where normal keyboard entry is neither possible nor desirable, such as in military systems where the hands might be doing something else, in warehouse systems to fetch the required goods to complete an order, or for those with disabilities which prevent normal keyboard use. However, groups such as the blind are unlikely to benefit since Braille keyboards have long been available and are easy to use for blind users. In early 1995 IBM launched its own Voice type system combining both dictation and control systems, although it can't deal with continuous natural speech, and has problems dealing with stuttering. Accuracy rates of 95% are claimed for the system.

Question 3.5

Distinguish between control and dictation systems.

Speech recognition involves four main stages: converting speech to digital code, analysing the code, interpreting the meaning and making an appropriate response. Computer speech systems don't necessarily deal with all four stages.

Analogue to digital converters (ADCs) can be used to sample and digitise speech, and in essence are no different from the technology used in recording music compact discs. However, a problem for modern speech recognition systems is that they often need to be combined with telephone technology to be effective, but the quality of the public telephone network is very limited and allows only a small sample of speech frequencies to be transmitted. So we need to establish whether a speech system is for use with the telephone network, in which case it must be able to deal with poor quality reduced frequency signals, or whether it can make use of higher quality signals.

Question 3.6

Why is the combination of speech recognition and telephone systems so important?

Analysing the digitised speech involves comparing the signals to a stored database of phonemes, which are the basic sound elements of natural speech. There are around 40 phonemes, corresponding to the basic sounds available in human natural language. For example, the speech synthesis program (not a recognition program) Monologue for Windows uses 43 phonetic codes to produce speech, representing sounds such as the ee sound in beet, the i sound in bit, the oo sound in book, the s sound in sin etc. Each sound is compared with the database of phonemes using a pattern matching algorithm to identify which phoneme it most closely resembles. Where there is ambiguity, or a failure to recognise, a good system will prompt the user, asking them to confirm 'that is oo as in boot' etc. A good pattern-matching algorithm will be able to cope with variations caused by accents, such as the differing pronunciation of the u in butter in the north and south of England (southerners pronounce it rather like the word batter, northerners like booter). The use of different words for the same object, such as boot and trunk to describe the rear luggage compartment of a car, needs to be considered when planning the vocabulary of the system. Typical conversational English uses around 10, 000 words, but specialist vocabularies may contain much more.

Philips Dictation Systems are currently working on speech recognition systems that will recognise continuous speech in specialist contexts, such as radiology. A major problem for recognition systems is knowing where one word or phoneme ends and the next begins, without requiring the user to speak in clipped artificial speech. The Philips system works by using statistical analysis of natural speech to predict the likelihood of the next word in the sentence given the context of use. Users can train the system in around 45 minutes by reading-in set texts. The vocabularies are typically around 25,000 words per context. The systems are particularly suitable for 'hands free, eyes free' tasks such as pathologists performing post-mortems, or automobile technicians reporting on vehicle engines during an inspection.

Having identified the phonemes, the resulting speech has to be analysed for meaning, using grammatical rules such as the requirement in English for a sentence to contain a subject, a verb and an object. This is not a simple task. Oracle have recently announced ConText, which they claim is the first package to analyse meaning. it took 18 years to develop, and contains a dictionary of 600,000 words linked to up to 1,000 pieces of linguistic data each. ConText allows intelligent searching of structured or unstructured data and the automatic analysis and summarising of textual information. However, an alternative technique is to use a limited context environment and to 'spot' certain words, for example the German railway system has an experimental speech recognition timetable enquiry system that allows users to phone up and ask the time of trains from one city to another. The system doesn't try to analyse all the spoken language, but to spot key words such as city names and days, dates etc. and to then make the appropriate response to the caller. Such keyword spotting is much simpler than a full semantic analysis of meaning.

The final stage, the production of an appropriate reply, is relatively simple compared with the previous stages. Speech synthesis systems either use pre-recorded samples of natural speech, from which they assemble an appropriate response, or they use text-to-speech synthesis similar to the programs that are often bundled with sound cards.

Question 3.7   Describe the four stages in speech systems.

The really major impact of speech recognition systems will be felt when they are capable of allowing telephone-based services such as enquiry and booking systems, direct insurance and sales to be replaced with speech recognition systems. However, at the moment it is too difficult to produce systems for answering calls from the general public, although there is scope currently for developing specialised systems for vertical markets such as the Philips system discussed earlier.

Answer 3.5

Control systems are relatively simple and only recognise a small number of pre-programmed commands such as 'Save', 'Print' etc. Dictation systems recognise continuous (more-or-less) natural speech, and at present are limited to specialised context systems such as the Philips Dictation system.

Answer 3.6

Because of the possibility of using computers to replace all those humans who answer the phone and deal with inquiries, bookings, sales etc. However, the impact on jobs in industries such as insurance, travel booking and inquires etc. are likely to be enormous.

Answer 3.7

Converting speech to machine-readable code, analysing the code into phonemes, analysing the meaning of the speech, and producing an appropriate response.

In summary, speech systems range from the relatively un-demanding synthesis of speech from text files, to systems that can respond to single commands, through to systems capable of analysing continuous speech and extracting meaning. Speech systems can be considered under the following broad headings:

- Single-word control systems

- Single speaker, continuous, limited vocabulary systems

- Single-speaker, continuous natural language systems

- Speaker-independent systems that can analyse continuous speech and meaning and make meaningful responses. Such systems could, in principle, have enormous impact if they could be used with telephone systems and the general public.

3.3 Output devices

3.3.1 Visual Display Units (VDUs)

These are by far the most common output device. Recent European and UK. legislation, and health fears over VDU use have lead to greater awareness of VDU ergonomics. Important considerations when choosing monitors include:

Size

Standard PC monitors are 14″ measured diagonally across the screen. This is fine for general tasks, but where you are working with graphics, for example using CAD or DTP software it may be necessary to use a larger size.

Magazine publishing in the UK typically uses A4 size paper, and journalists, editors and designers need to be able to see a full page, full size, on screen. This will require a 17″ monitor, which typically costs three to four times the price of a 14″ monitor.

The size required will also be related to the number of colours and pixels you want to display on screen. For a given size of monitor, a higher resolution will display more text etc. on screen, but it will be smaller and harder to read.

Mono or colour

For many applications, mono monitors are perfectly adequate, but others require colour. Word processing and database use is usually perfectly adequate on a mono monitor, however design and graphics work often requires colour. Many applications can benefit from the use of colour to draw attention to particular parts of the screen or screen objects, but colour can also be mis-used to produce garish and hard-to -read displays. Choosing inappropriate background and foreground colours for word processing, such as black text on a navy background, can make the text extremely difficult to read. Computer magazine advertisements can be a good source of examples of inappropriate colour choices! It is also important to remember that approximately 8% of males are colour blind (but only 1% of females). A very brief guide to using colour in the design of interfaces is included with Microsoft Visual Basic 3 for Windows, in the Learning Visual Basic tutorial section on 'Using colour and graphics'.

Number of colours

For many applications, 16 colours are sufficient. However, designers who need natural colour will need 256 colours as a minimum, and possibly true colour (16 million colours or 24-bit colour).

Resolution

Resolution is a measure of the number of pixels that make up the screen. The higher the number, the better the resolution. Common resolutions are currently:

- VGA 640 X480,
- SVGA 800 X 600,
- XVGA (8514) 1024 X 768 pixels.

Earlier standards include EGA 640 X 350, CGA 320 X 200 and Hercules (mono) 720 X 320, but these standards are now obsolete.

Scanning frequency

This refers to the speed with which the electron beam passes from one side of the screen to the other (horizontal) or the number of complete screens scanned per second. It is important for minimizing screen flicker. Vertical scanning frequencies should be at least 60 Hz for all the resolutions above. Horizontal scanning frequencies should be at least 35.1 KHz for VGA and above displays.

Interlaced/non-interlaced

Interlacing is a way of scanning lines where the odd-numbered lines are scanned first, then the even ones. It allows faster scanning rates, but interlaced monitors produce more flicker, especially at higher resolutions. Non-interlaced monitors produce the steadiest image, but cost more. Since one of the EEC 90/270 requirements is for flicker-free displays, it is safest to choose non-interlaced monitors for SVGA resolutions and above.

Dot pitch

This is a measure of the sharpness of the image. The smaller the dot pitch, the sharper the image. A dot pitch of 0.31mm or less is typical for current monitors.

Display card

As well as the monitor itself, you also need to consider the specification of the display card that 'drives' it. A 16 colour SVGA display needs 4 bits of memory for each pixel, making 1,920,000 bits (800 x 600 x 4). A 256Kb video card will be more than sufficient (1,920,000 divide by 8 =240,000). However, if 256 colour (8-bit) SVGA is required, more memory will be needed on the video card (480Kb). 1Mb is a realistic minimum for colour graphics work currently.

Question 3.8

What factors need to be considered when selecting monitors for:

- DTP colour publishing
- word processing.

3.3.2 Microfilm

Output to microfilm was a popular way of storing data such as newspapers. It is a photographic technique, and a special viewer is needed to view the film. The British Library newspaper division, which keeps copies of all newspapers published in Britain, uses microfilm storage. It is easy to use with an appropriate viewer.

3.3.3 Microfiche

Microfiche is in effect simply microfilm cut up into pieces. It is often used in car parts departments and in libraries, for example, for British Standards publications. It requires a simple viewer to view the fiche. We can expect that increasingly CD-ROM will replace microfilm and fiche, with several newspapers now available on CD-ROM

3.3.4 CD-ROM Devices

As mentioned above, CD-ROM is replacing microfilm and fiche. Sony now produce miniature CD-ROM data discs and discman-type portable devices that allow the 'reading' of electronic 'books' on a device about the same size as a Walkman, with no need for bulky PCs with CD-ROM drives. Early newspaper CD-ROMs were often text-only. Just like any other software, CD-ROM software interfaces need careful design for good usability.

3.3.5 Printers

The question of suitable type of printer is quite complex, with the need to take account not just of the quality required, whether colour printing is required, the size required of printed output, but also factors such as volume and speed, operating environments, limitations on noise levels etc. As a general rule, use Dot-matrix for multi-part forms and for draft quality output, ink jet for low volume and portable high quality output, and laser jet for correspondence quality output. Colour is available using the above technologies plus thermal wax transfer. Production of overhead projector slides may be done on ink jet or laser printers, but requires special film. Braille printers allow output that can be read by the blind. Many printers have a range of very poorly designed controls and error messages that often allow end users to unwittingly change print options. Ease of use for tasks such as label and envelope printing also varies enormously, as does the range of papers and card that can be used successfully.

3.3.6 Video

Computer data can be output to video to enable the viewing of multimedia training materials on ordinary video recorders, which are generally easy to use for playback. Moving video output to PCs is an important component of video conferencing systems such as Intel's ProShare Personal Video Conferencing system. Such systems combine groupware software, miniature video cameras and ISDN telephone links to provide the high bandwidth required for moving video. ISDN telephone lines aren't required for videoconferencing over high bandwidth local area networks. See Chapter 6 for more on groupware systems.

3.3.7 Virtual Reality headsets

These use miniature screens to provide 3-D effects, together with stereo speakers. They are currently being marketed with virtual reality games software, but have many potential serious uses. They can be thought of as lightweight, personal simulators.

3.3.8 Sound

Speech synthesis software often comes bundled free with sound cards, and can for example, take a piece of text from the windows clipboard and turn it into (rather artificial sounding) speech. Speech output is much simpler than speech input, and is a useful alternative to Braille printers for the blind. Speech is of course also useful in multi-media output, since material presented to human users through more than one channel has greater impact than single-channel output. However, CD-quality digitised sound requires around 10 Mb of memory per minute; a 650 Mb compact disc can only contain just over one hour of sound. If speech dialogue only is required, for example in a spoken commentary or instruction, then 8-bit mono sampling at 11.025KHz is acceptable, giving file sizes of 645 Kb per minute. With compression techniques such as TrueSpeech, this can be reduced to 62Kb per minute. Many systems can only deal with very short (4 second) speech clips where speech and images need to be synchronised, as a result of the high data transfer rates needed with speech output.

3.3.9 Electronic output

We shouldn't forget that data can be output to disks etc. Sometimes it is appropriate to output data to storage devices or via communication links to other computers, as in Email systems. It is much easier to give someone a floppy and directions to another office than to teach them to use a file transfer program, null modem cable or Email system.

3.4 Interaction styles

These can be broadly classified into command language, menu-based, direct manipulation, natural language, question-and-answer and form-fill.

3.4.1 Command-language interfaces

Until the 1980s most interfaces required the user to type in precise instructions such as

'LIST TO PRINT'

in order to carry-out tasks. The problem with such a dialogue style was that the syntax had to be precise, with no additional or missed spaces or punctuation, otherwise the command wouldn't work. Such a dialogue style also required the user to memorise large numbers of complex command sequences.

For colour DTP work you should specify at least a 17" monitor (for A4 work), with the ability to deal with true (24-bit) colour. Non-interlaced fine dot-pitch monitors and graphics cards with plenty of memory will also be required. Word processing is much less critical in its demands, and doesn't even require a colour monitor.

However, research in psychology has shown that humans are much better at recognising the correct command from a list of commands on a menu than they are at recalling precise syntax from memory, and this is why menu-based applications became very popular in the 1980s. Probably the ultimate minimalist command-language interface was the dBase 'dot-prompt' interface: the interface consisted of a blank screen with just a full stop in the bottom left corner of the screen with a blinking cursor alongside. No other information was provided at all to the user. The MS-DOS interface is similarly minimalist, consisting typically of the following:

C:>

Commands such as dir, type etc. are entered at this prompt.

3.4.2 Menus

As we saw above, recognising the correct command from a menu is easier than recalling it from memory, hence the popularity of menu-based interfaces in the 1980s. For example, in some software the command to leave the program is quit, in others, exit. With a command-driven system, you have to remember which it is (along with any other necessary detail such as whether it should be in upper or lower case etc.). With a menu-based system, you only have to select the command from the menu.

A further benefit of menus is that you can usually select the appropriate option just by pressing one key, for example, in Word for windows you can select Print Preview from the File menu just by pressing the V key rather than having to type out 'PRINT PREVIEW'. Such keystroke shortcuts are extremely useful to allow experienced users to work more quickly, and should be provided for all common tasks such as saving, printing etc.

There are several ways menus can be implemented:

Cascading: e.g. in many applications, selecting an option from a menu calls up a further menu. If a menu contains too many items it is inefficient. Cascading menus reduce the items and group logically-related items together.

Fixed: menu remains in place.

Pop-up and drop-down menus. In the Windows interface, selecting the File menu with a mouse causes the menu to drop-down. However, selecting the Open option from the menu causes a dialog-box to pop-up. The database package dBase IV makes extensive use of pop-up menus.

Menuing systems can also make use of colour coding to highlight important information, such as the greying-out of non-available commands in Windows applications, and grouping of related items to make it easier to find the required action, for example all the printing options such as Print, Preview, Print Merge and Print Set-up should be grouped together.

A typical drop-down menu style: Windows Write. Note that non-available options are greyed-out.

Potential *problems* with menus include consideration of what items to include in them, and how to group them. Groupings should be consistent with other applications where possible-consult the relevant style guide for the 'rules' for your particular interface. Possible ways to group items are alphabetical, by category (e.g. all the formatting options on one menu, file operations on another etc.), and frequency of use, with all the most frequently performed actions together. It is also a good idea to keep separate opposite actions such as saving and deleting, since it is all too easy to select the wrong item, particularly for inexperienced mouse users, with potentially disastrous (and de-motivating) consequences.

Question 3.9

If possible, obtain copies of different applications packages and compare the menu structures, for example Lotus 1-2-3 for DOS and Supercalc for DOS, Superbase 4 for Windows and Access. Which packages heave the better designed menu structures?

Question 3.10

Design menu structures for the following applications:

(a) college student enrolment database

(b) order database for a supplier of office equipment

3.4.3 Natural language dialogue

In natural language systems, rather than entering commands or selecting from menus more-or-less natural language can be used to interact with the system, for example a train timetable inquiry system could be used by typing in 'when is the next train from Manchester to Birmingham?'. Natural language systems should not be confused with speech recognition systems. In a natural language system input is still normally via the keyboard, e.g. the Eliza program which simulates a consultation with a Rogerian psychotherapist (don't worry if you aren't sure about these terms-ask a counsellor!). the user types in anything they like. Eliza searches for certain patterns and key words and then replies, usually in a quite convincing style, for example the user might type in 'I often feel lacking in energy' to which Eliza might reply 'Why do you say that you lack energy?' and so on.

Natural language systems are often combined with speech recognition to provide simple command and control systems, such as are discussed in the section on speech recognition in this chapter. The Apple and Windows operating systems both had such natural language control systems available as add-ons.

3.4.4 Question and answer

As its name suggests, this dialogue style presents the user with an on-screen question, perhaps in the form of a checklist or questionnaire, with a space for them to type-in their reply. Such systems can be used, for example, for on-screen VDU health and safety questionnaires as part of an audit procedure to comply with the UK Display Screen Equipment Regulations.

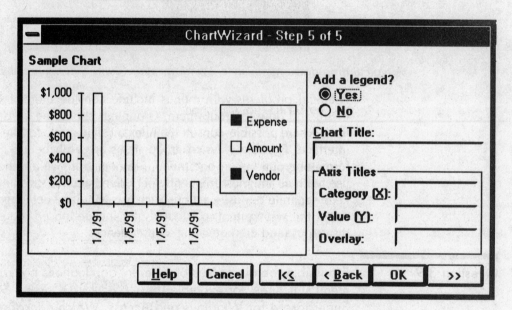

Example of question-and-answer form from Microsoft Excel

3.4.5 Form-fill

Form-fill is similar to the above style, with on-screen 'documents' designed as far as possible to mimic the paper ones that they replace. Many database packages allow the design of custom forms for data entry, with the 'answers' being stored as fields in a database. Examples include the form design features available in Microsoft Access.

The interface style of many of the latest generation of Microsoft's own application packages such as Publisher, Access and Excel often make use of form-fill in the form of the so-called 'wizards' that take the user step-by-step through common tasks such as designing a calendar or a database.

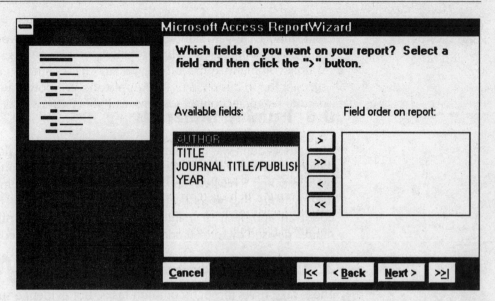

Example of form-fill dialogue style: Microsoft Access Wizard

3.4.6 Direct manipulation

Performing operations such as moving a file by clicking on an icon representing the file and dragging it to a new location, e.g. moving a file from drive C to A in the Windows File Manager. Direct manipulation typically involves a WIMP environment (Windows, Icons, Mouse, Pointing), also known as GUIs or graphical user interfaces. Note that an interface can be a GUI or WIMP interface without necessarily making use of direct manipulation, although the two do tend to go hand-in-hand.

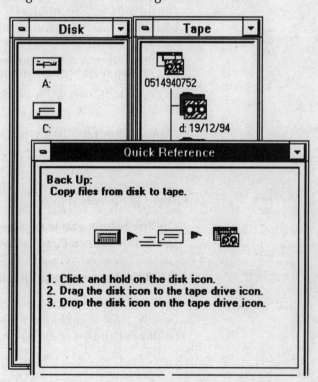

Example of a direct-manipulation interface. Backing-up a disk in Colorado Lite is achieved by clicking on the drive icon and dragging it to the tape icon.

Question3.11 Distinguish between menu-based, question-and-answer, form-fill and direct manipulation interface styles.

3.5 Training materials

Many users don't want to read long, complicated manuals, and evidence suggests that they don't read them until they get stuck. On-line support forums often have a special section called RTFM which stands for read the flippin manual! However, it's best to acknowledge that users prefer to get stuck in without reading the manual, and to adopt an approach to manual writing based on the minimalist instructional techniques devised by Carroll and others (these are discussed more fully in Chapter 9).

3.5.1 Computerised demonstrations and 'tutorials'

These take users through common tasks, but evidence suggests that because of their passive nature, users are unlikely to remember much of the procedures described. They are however useful for giving the user a quick introduction to the interface. If users are only required to retain information on how to use the system long enough to perform a single task, then such approaches can be useful, but they are not suitable for those who have to learn the system for regular use.

3.5.2 Help and reference information

Printed command and action references, with examples are generally a good idea, especially for those familiar with similar software. There should be cross-referencing since many actions are given different names by different users e.g. converting files could be the same action as importing or exporting files, or using xyz files. It is important to get a list of names that users typically use for particular actions and to ensure that the action is listed under each heading rather than under just one. Research has shown that if you list a particular operation under the five most common terms used to describe it, over 80% of users will be able to find it under one or other of those terms.

Manuals are only likely to be turned to when users get stuck, rather than when learning the system. There should be several different types of manual, for example a 'Getting started' introduction, tutorial manuals, quick reference information and comprehensive reference manuals. Chapter 9 goes into manuals in greater depth. There is a British Standard, BS 7649, on the production of software documentation.

On-line help is also used when users get stuck, and to look up the syntax for particular actions. The facility to obtain print-outs of selected help topics is very useful.

3.5.3 Customer support helplines

Most vendors provide some system of telephone support for registered users, although usually there is a charge for such support after an initial free period. Such support helplines can be a useful source of feedback from users concerning usability issues.

Answer to 3.11

Menus only require the user to recognise the correct option from the displayed list. Question-and-answer interfaces require, typically, yes or no answers to on-screen prompts. Form-fill interfaces require the user to complete certain items of information, usually by keying in text. Direct-manipulation interfaces require the user to use 'drag and drop' or similar techniques.

3.5.4 On-line forums on Compuserve, the Internet etc.

Many hardware and software vendors provide support on the Internet, through Usenet Newsgroups or through Compuserve forums. Currently there are over 500 forums on Compuserve alone providing support, from companies such as IBM, Microsoft, Apple, Intel, Lotus etc. At the moment, it is reasonable to assume that any user using such help is likely to be fairly experienced in computer use, although not necessarily in the particular product. Requests for assistance from users are left in the form of an email message, which the forum or newsgroup replies to by email. Once such a service is provided, it can be used by developers to analyse the kinds of problems users are having and to provide a 'frequently asked questions' section in the newsgroup or forum, as well as providing important data for the next upgrade of the system!

Review questions

1. Why should standard keyboards be our first choice of input device?

2. Why isn't moving video used more in systems?

3. How does videoconferencing solve some of the problems of traditional Email systems?

4. Why is speech input so difficult?

5. How can the input and output needs of users with special needs best be met?

6. Why should command-language interfaces generally be avoided?

Test questions

1. Discuss the potential benefits and problems of using speech input systems.

2. Evaluate the different types of interaction dialogue, giving examples of applications for which each interaction style is particularly suited.

3. What special issues do multimedia systems raise compared with single-channel input and output such as traditional VDU displays?

4 Standards and the law

Introduction

In this chapter we shall be looking at national and international standards affecting interface design, European Union directives on health and safety aspects of working with computer systems, on legal issues affecting the design and use of systems and on the conformance testing of systems to ensure compliance with legislation and standards.

- International HCI standards
- International Standards Organisation ISO 9241
- Software documentation standards: BS 7649
- Other ergonomic standards
- Health and safety at work requirements
- Display Screen Equipment Regulations EEC 90/270
- Usability and software ergonomics
- Conformance with standards and compliance testing
- Legal issues when distributing software
- Copyright law and the interface-the Copyright, Design and patents Act 1988
- The Computer Misuse Act 1990
- The Data Protection Act 1984

4.1 International HCI standards

The European Commission Directive on 'Minimum Health and Safety Requirements for Work with Display Screen Equipment' EEC 90/270, which became law in the UK on 1 January 1993, contains minimum ergonomic requirements for computing equipment, the environment and the human-computer interface. The directive requires that 'The software must be easy to use' and 'The principles of software ergonomics must be applied'. While various national standards exist covering different aspects of systems ergonomics, ISO 9241 is being developed as a multi-part international standard with a similar scope to the directive and which will spell-out in detail the general requirement for ease of use of systems. It is expected that by the mid to late 1990s the standard will be published in final form and conformance with the standard will be a legal requirement in all EEC countries. Early drafts of the parts of the standard concerned with software ergonomics (part 10) have also found widespread acceptance among HCI experts in North America, Japan, and Australia as well as Europe.

4.1.1 Software ergonomics requirements of EEC 90/270

- Software must be suitable for the task, allowing users to complete tasks efficiently without presenting unnecessary problems or obstacles.

- Easy to use. The software should be easy to learn, intuitive, and appropriate to the user's ability.

- The system's speed of response to commands and instructions should be immediately shown on screen, and should be appropriate to the task and the worker's abilities.

- Adaptable to the operator's skill level. Experienced users should be able to adapt the interface to suit their particular ability level and preferences.

- The software should prevent users from errors and allow error recovery.

- No quantitative or qualitative testing, such as measuring output speed, should be carried out without the operator being informed that such testing is taking place.

- Systems must give VDU workers feedback on their performance. Such feedback should be in an appropriate style and format, and should not contain unnecessary information. Help facilities should be provided.

Question 4.1

Draw up a checklist of the above requirements from EEC 90/270 and use it to carry out an evaluation of the extent to which a software package meets the requirements. You may find it useful to use some type of five-point scale (e.g. 1 for 'poor'. 5 for 'excellent') for each of the points in the box above.

4.1.2 ISO 9241

ISO 9241 is an emerging standard on ergonomic requirements for office work with visual display terminals (VDTs). There will eventually be 17 parts to the standard. Part 10 of the standard is the part dealing with software ergonomics and usability, and is currently at the draft stage. Several earlier parts of the standard have already been incorporated within British Standards, such as BS 7169 and EN 29241 but are concerned mainly with hardware aspects of VDT design.

ISO 9241 parts

1. General introduction
2. Guidance on task requirements
3. Visual display requirements
4. Keyboard requirements
5. Workstation layout requirements
6. Environmental requirements
7. Display requirements with reflections
8. Requirements for displayed colours
9. Requirements for non-keyboard input devices

10. Dialogue principles

11. Usability statements

12. Presentation of information

13. User guidance

14. Menu dialogues

15. Command dialogues

16. Direct manipulation dialogues

17. Form filling dialogues

Since computer users engage in 'dialogues' with computers, part 10 of the standard focuses on the design of such dialogues, which include the use of:

• menus

• command languages

• natural language

• form-based entry

• question-and-answer

• direct manipulation of icons and objects.

It identifies the following seven principles for dialogue design:

1. Suitability for the task

2. Self-descriptiveness

3. Controllability

4. Conformity with user expectations

5. Error tolerance

6. Suitability for individualization

7. Suitability for learning.

The precise way in which the principles should be applied needs to take account of the characteristics of users, their tasks and the operating environment of the system. The overall approach in the principles is to take a user-centred approach to design.

Part 11 of the standard is concerned with measuring software usability, and work is in hand to develop software that will allow a piece of software to be tested to see if it complies with the ISO 9241 standard or not. Since it is expected that conformance with the standard will be part of the requirements specification of all new systems and software, this is obviously going to become a very important area of work. Software developers and buyers of software will both need to take into account the standard's requirements and will need practical ways to measure conformance.

The International Standards Organisation propose that

> "The usability of a product is the degree to which specific users can achieve specific goals within a particular environment; effectively, efficiently, comfortably, and in an acceptable manner." (Booth 1989 p110).

4.1.3 BS 7649: Design of Documentation for users of applications software.

BS 7649, produced in 1993, contains around 90 pages of detailed information about documentation design. The standard is discussed more fully in chapter seven.

BS 7649 recommends the following approach:

- Collect details of users and tasks
- Determine users' documentation needs
- Record users' information needs
- Produce the documentation plan

User information should be collected under the following headings:

- Types of user: level of computing experience, knowledge of system, cultural and linguistic factors etc.

- Tasks: make a list of the typical tasks that real users perform, then construct Storyboards of typical task scenarios, using cognitive walkthrough techniques (discussed further in Chapter 6.)

- Learning stages: the way that users' performance is expected to change over time as they use the system.

- Environments: what hardware is available, is the environment especially dirty, oily, dusty, humid, hot or cold etc., is there suitable space for software manuals etc.

BS 7649 regards the following items as essential for all software:

- Document reference number
- Product model, type and version
- Document title, including product name
- Date of issue
- Version number of the document
- Name, address, telephone, fax and Email details of the product supplier and, where different, the document publisher

General points on documentation writing style

- Use a simple style, but don't patronise.

- Divide text into short sections with clear section headings and appropriate use of white space. Jokes should be avoided. Humour and cartoons may be appropriate, but avoid any culture bias. Humour often does not translate well across cultures, and may accidentally offend.

- Complex ideas should be broken-down into simpler components

- Warnings should be given in the imperative- for example, the command 'Stop!' which sometimes appears when using Windows.

- Illustrations, lists and tables should be used where they better convey ideas than text, or help to clarify the text. They also help to break-up the text.

4.1.4 Other ergonomic standards

ISO 9241 is based on various earlier standards such as the German DIN 66234. The German TV Ergonomie Gepruft standard for monitors covers both radiation and general ergonomics. UK health and safety at work legislation, especially the Health And Safety At Work Act 1974, lays down safety-related ergonomic requirements covering such issues as lighting, temperature etc.

British Standard BS 7179 is concerned with the ergonomics of the design and use of visual display terminals in offices and is in six parts, but these are gradually being superseded by EN 29241 (the British Standards Institute catalogue number for ISO 9241). Most earlier standards had little to say about software ergonomics.

Question 4.2   What are the most important standards covering software ergonomics?

4.2 Health and safety at work: general requirements

These are laid-down in the Health And Safety At Work Act 1974, and the Management of Health And Safety At Work Act 1992. Both are concerned with the provision of safe systems of work and work environments. Although important, they don't address questions of interface design.

4.3 Display Screen Equipment Regulations EEC 90/270

These Regulations declare that all new workstations introduced after 1 January 1993, and all existing workstations from 1 January 1997 must comply with the requirements of the regulations.

Question 4.3   What are the main dialogue requirements of ISO 9241?

4.3.1 Who is covered by the legislation?

Those covered by the legislation are people habitually using display screen equipment including alpha-numeric or graphic display screens regardless of the display process involved. These come under two categories; 'operator' means a self employed person who habitually uses display screen equipment as a significant part of their every day work, 'user' means an employee who habitually uses screen equipment as a significant part of his or her every day work.

In some cases it would be clear that use of display screen equipment is more or less continuous on most days and the individuals concerned should be regarded as users or operators. This will include the majority of those whose job mainly involves, for example, display screen based data input or sales and order processing. Where use is less continuous or frequent, other factors connected with the job must be assessed. It will generally be appropriate to classify the person concerned as a user or operator if most or all of the following criteria apply.

4.3.2 Definition of a user or operator

1. the individual depends on the use of display screen equipment to do the job, as alternative means are not readily available for achieving the same results;

Answer 4.2	ISO 9241
Answer 4.3	1. *Suitability for the task*
	2. *Self-descriptiveness*
	3. *Controllability*
	4. *Conformity with user expectations*
	5. *Error tolerance*
	6. *Suitability for individualization*
	7. *Suitability for learning.*

2. the individual has no discretion as to use or non-use of the display screen equipment;

3. the individual needs significant training and/or particular skills in the use of display screen equipment to do the job;

4. the individual normally uses display screen equipment for continuous spells of an hour or more at a time;

5. the individual uses display screen equipment in this way more or less daily;

6. fast transfer of information between the user and screen is an important requirement of the job;

7. the performance requirements of the system demand high levels of attention and concentration by the user, for example, where the consequences of error may be critical.

4.3.3 Examples of typical display screen jobs

• Secretary or typist who uses word processing system.

• Data input operator on continuous processing of invoices.

• News sub-editor making use of display screen equipment more or less continuously.

• Journalistic work may be varied but includes substantial use of display screen equipment.

• Graphic designer working on multi-media applications.

• Tele-sales/customer complaints/accounts enquiries/directory inquiries operator.

Examples of possible display screen users:

• Client manager in a large management accounting consultancy, typically one and a half to two hours daily use of display screen equipment.

• Airline check-in clerk using display screen equipment as part of most transactions, but who does not use VDUs for significant proportion of total working time.

• Receptionist.

Examples that would definitely not be classed as display screen users:

- Senior manager in a large organisation using display screen for occasional monitoring of state of markets or other data.

- Receptionist if work is mainly concerned with customer/public interaction with occasional use of VDUs for obtaining details of telephone numbers, location, etc.

Question 4.4

Who is covered by the Display Screen Equipment 90/270 regulations?

4.3.4 Requirements of the directive

Employers must:

- Carry out a full audit of all equipment to assess possible risks to workers' eyesight, and risks of physical problems and stress. Steps must be taken to remedy any problems.

- Make sure that any workstations put into service for the first time from 1 January 1993 meet with the requirements. Those already in service must conform no later than 31 December 1996.

- Provide employees with information on all aspects of health and safety when using a workstation.

- Training must be provided before commencing this type of work or whenever the organisation is substantially modified.

- Build regular breaks or changes of activity into the work routine to reduce the workload at the screen.

- Consult with employee representatives on all aspects of health and safety when using a workstation

- Provide eye tests for any employee commencing VDU work, at regular intervals thereafter, or if problems arise. If special glasses are required as a result, the employer must provide them.

4.3.5 Detailed requirements

Screens

- Well-defined characters of adequate size and spacing.

- A stable image with no flickering

- Easily adjustable brightness and contrast controls

- Tilt and swivel base

- Free from reflective glare.

Keyboards

- Tiltable and separable from the screen.

- Enough space in front to rest hands and arms.

- Matt non-reflective surface.

- Key symbols must be clear and legible.

Answer 4.4   *Users, whether employees or self-employed contractors, and including those working from home, who depend on a VDU to do their work, and who work at VDUs for continuous spells of an hour or more each day. See above.*

Work desk/ work surface

- Large and non-reflective surface.

- Document holders must be stable and positioned to minimise head and eye movements.

Work chair

- Must be stable and allow easy movement.

- Seat height and height and tilt of back must be adjustable.

- A footrest must be available to anyone who wants one.

Environment

- Enough space must be available to allow operators to change position and vary movements.

- Lighting, both artificial and from windows, should be arranged to minimise glare and provide sufficient contrast between the screen and background environment.

- Adjustable blinds must be fitted to the windows.

- Noise from other equipment shouldn't disturb speech or distract attention.

- Heat and radiation emissions from equipment should be kept to a minimum.

- Adequate humidity should be maintained.

Operator/computerinterface

- Software must be suitable for the task, allowing users to complete tasks efficiently without presenting unnecessary problems or obstacles.

- Easy to use. The software should be easy to learn, intuitive, and appropriate to the user's ability.

- Adaptable to the operator's skill level. Experienced users should be able to adapt the interface to suit their particular ability level and preferences.

- The software should prevent users from errors and allow error recovery.

- No qualitative testing must be carried out without the operator's permission.

- Systems must give VDU workers feedback on their performance. Such feedback should be in an appropriate style and format, and should not contain unnecessary information. Help facilities should be provided.

4.3.6 Daily work routine of users

Every employer should plan the activities of users at work so that their daily work on display screen equipment is periodically interrupted by such breaks or changes of activity in order to reduce their workload at that equipment.

In most tasks, natural breaks or pauses occur as an inherent part of the work. Whenever possible, jobs at display screens should be designed to consist of a mix of screen-based and non screen-based work to prevent fatigue and to vary visual and mental demands. Where the job unavoidably contains spells of intensive display screen work (whether using the keyboard or input devices, reading the screen or a mixture of the two), these should be broken up by periods of non-intensive, non-display screen work. For example, periodically getting up to go to a store cupboard to obtain paper to load a printer etc.

Where work cannot be so organised, e.g. in jobs requiring only data or text entry requiring sustained attention and concentration, deliberate breaks or pauses must be introduced.

Nature and timing of breaks or changes of activity

Where the display screen work involves intensive use of the keyboard, any activity that would demand broadly similar use of the arms or hands should be avoided during breaks. Similarly, if the display screen work is visually demanding any activities during breaks should be of a different visual character. Breaks must also allow users to vary their posture. Exercise routines that include blinking, stretching and focusing eyes on distant objects can be helpful and could be covered in training programmes.

It is not appropriate to lay down requirements for breaks that apply to all types of work; it is the nature and mix of demands made by the job which determine the length of break necessary to prevent fatigue. But some general guidance can be given:

- Breaks should be taken before the onset of fatigue, and when performance is at a maximum, before productivity reduces. The timing of the break is more important then its length.

- Breaks or changes of activity should be included in working time. They should reduce the workload at the screen, i.e. should not result in a higher pace or intensity of work on account of their introduction. They don't need to be scheduled 'tea breaks'.

- Short, frequent breaks are more satisfactory than occasional, longer breaks: e.g., a 5–10 minute break after 50–60 minutes of continuous screen and/or keyboard work is likely to be better than a 15 minute break every 2 hours.

- If possible, breaks should be taken away from the screen. Users should be discouraged, for example, from eating their lunch in front of a VDU.

- Informal breaks, that is time spent not viewing the screen (e.g. on other tasks), appear from the evidence to be more effective in relieving visual fatigue than formal rest breaks.

- Whenever practicable, users should be allowed some discretion as to how they carry out tasks; individual control over the nature and pace of work allows optimal distribution of effort over the working day.

Question 4.5

You have been asked by a small company with 50 employees, half of whom use VDUs, to design an on-screen checklist that can be used to carry out workstation assessments in order to comply with the requirements of DSE 90/270. Design and implement such a system in a database package or programming language of your choice. Your system should comply with the requirements for software ergonomics and meet the risk assessment requirements of the regulations. It is suggested that it take the form of an on-screen checklist, the answers to which can then be stored in, for example, the fields of a database file.

4.4 Usability and software ergonomics

Usability has become the software industry buzz-word for the 90's. A number of major PC software houses have turned their backs on the 'feature wars', and announced their intention of concentrating instead on how usable their products are. Microsoft, in particular, has announced that features increasingly packed into their software have not always made them any easier to use.

The EC have declared in EEC 90/270 that "Software Must Be Suitable For The Task, Easy To Use And Flexible To The Operator's Skill Level".

The UK department of trade and industry(DTI) are concerned with usability of systems. To promote more usable systems in the late 80's it launched a campaign called 'Usability Now!'. The DTI say that usable systems are safe, comfortable, efficient, easy and maybe even enjoyable to use. Before the DTI approves a system it looks for:

- Consideration of the users needs during the functional specification - with the aid of formal design techniques.

- Attention to type, style and detail of the user interface.

- A usable working environment, taking into account health, comfort and ergonomic factors, Organisation, job design and learning/training.

- Use of prototyping concepts and techniques to refine and confirm the design, and evaluation of the design in operation.

- The DTI also suggests that the system must be considered throughout its lifetime.

Here are some examples of how usability can be improved:

- In Microsoft Word the old 'cut and paste' method of moving blocks of text has been developed into dragging and dropping. This design proved successful after extensive usability research.

- Most users don't want to change settings, so research should establish the most useful default settings and provide quick access to the most used functions (for example, the sum function in Excel is accessed just by clicking on the sum symbol on the toolbar).

- Icons should be realistic in the context of their use. In early versions of Excel the piggy bank symbol was used for saving work, but usability research showed that users didn't associate the idea of saving their data to the idea of saving money so the icon was changed to a 3.5 in floppy disk.

Question 4.6　　Draw up a checklist of the points that the UK's DTI looks for before approving a system.

Evidence of user consultation.
Evidence of use of formal design techniques.
Evidence of use of prototyping and user feedback.
Evidence that context, workplace organisation, training needs etc. have been taken into account.

4.5 Conformance with standards: conformance testing of software

Once finalised versions of standards such as ISO 9241 are in place, all software will be capable of being tested to assess the extent to which it conforms to standard. Work is already under way to develop conformance testing software, notably the EVADIS II software designed to test conformance with ISO 9241 which is under development at the German National research Centre for Computer Science. Similar work is also under way at the National Physical Laboratory at Teddington, Middlesex. Less formal methods of testing the usability of software have been developed by a number of organisations, including software designers, hardware manufacturers and publishers such as Ziff-Davis. Methods of usability testing are surveyed in Chapter 6.

4.6 Legal issues when distributing systems

4.6.1 Copyright law and the interface

The law of copyright applies to computer software in much the same way that it applies to books and other materials. You can't copyright an idea, only the expression of that idea. For example, you may write some software to measure the correct amount of hair colouring to use in a hairdressing salon. You can't use copyright law to prevent others from writing similar software to measure amounts of hair colour, but you can protect your own specific implementation of the idea (your own actual code) if you can prove that the other company simply copied your code.

- Computer software is protected automatically under the Copyright, Design and Patents Act 1988, although it is sensible to post a copy of the software to an independent third party such as a firm of solicitors in order to prove that it existed at a particular time in the event of a later dispute about copyright. It is also common to include some nonsense code that will show up on any unauthorised copy, and the use of serial numbers so that you can trace unauthorised copies to particular license holders (who can then be held liable for the unlawful copying).

- Copyright normally belongs to the author of the software, unless the author is employed specifically to write software in which case it normally belongs to the company. An employee who writes a useful program for the company in his or her own time would normally retain copyright, but individual employment contracts can alter these normal copyright arrangements.

- Copyright protection makes it unlawful to copy the software or to change or adapt it. However, licensed users have the right to make a backup copy and to make minor necessary alterations for example to overcome a bug in the program.

Question 4.7

You are employed as a software developer to write database applications for clients. You write such an application in your spare time for one of your company's clients. Do you own the copyright?

4.6.2 Copyright and shareware, on-line databases and public domain software

Material downloaded from information providers such as those on Compuserve are subject to the normal copyright laws, with in the main short extracts being free of copyright restrictions. Shareware programs should be licensed, but public domain software does not require a license.

4.6.3 Software licensing

It is now increasingly common for users to want to use software in the office, on a machine at home and possibly on a laptop. Whether such use is allowed depends on the wording of the specific license, with different software vendors adopting differing policies on the issue.

- Individual licensed user can use the software on any machines they like providing only one copy of the software is in use at anyone time.

- Individual licensed user can make a second copy for use on either a laptop or home machine, but not both.

- Individual licensed user can only use on one specific machine.

- Site licences: these usually require an annual fee in return for unlimited copying and use at a single site.

- Volume licenses: these are more suitable for multi-site organisations such as many public sector organisations, and allow a specified number or unlimited numbers of users throughout the organization, regardless of site. They may allow use on unlimited numbers of workstations on a LAN, but allow only a specified number of concurrent users.

Question 4.8

I am an authorised user of 'Shutters for windows' at work. Can I copy the software and use it on my home machine?

4.6.4 Disposing/reselling of software and upgrades

Where a company or individual upgrades its equipment, the license may or may not allow the transfer of software to other users. However, it is definitely not allowed to buy an upgrade package and sell the old version of the software.

4.6.5 Software piracy

Unauthorised copying of software breaks both the civil and criminal law. The Copyright, Design and Patents Act 1988 makes it a criminal offence to possess in the course of a business an article which infringes copyright. Penalties are up to six months imprisonment and a fine of up to £5,000 for criminal breaches of the law.

Answer 4.7   *This could be a legal minefield. All employees should look at their contracts of employment to see what they have to say on the matter of copyright, since practice varies widely. Generally, engaging in the same business as you employer with one of your employer's clients is likely to constitute a breach of faith and could even constitute grounds for dismissal! If you're employed specifically to write software your contract of employment is likely to deal explicitly with the issue.*

Answer 4.8   *You can only be sure by checking the terms of your licensing agreement to see if it allows such use.*

Additionally, the copyright owner can sue for damages in the civil courts, both from the person possessing the pirated software and from the holder of the licence of the software that has been copied. When you fill in your name to register software you are identifying yourself as the holder of a licence to use that software. The licence terms make you liable to damages in the event of piracy. The Federation against Software Theft (FAST) regularly organises raids on organisations suspected of piracy, and can use the courts to gain powers of entry and seizure of equipment.

To remain within the law organisations need clear policies against piracy, with centralised recording of software licenses held and machines where they may be legally used. Some licenses permit software to be installed on machines at work and home, provided only one is in use at any one time. There is also auditing software available which can be used to obtain details of software that has been installed on a machine until recently: quickly erasing pirate software as FAST arrives won't avoid detection, damages and prosecution. Employers should make software piracy by employees a disciplinary offence, in order to get across the message concerning its illegality and also to cover themselves against claims for damages and the risk of prosecution.

Question 4.9   What precautions against liability for software piracy should an organization take?

4.6.6 Computer Misuse Act 1990: computer hacking

This act makes it a criminal offence to move, copy, alter or erase a computer program without authorised access. Offenders face fines and imprisonment as well as civil proceedings for damages. The legislation is aimed at hackers and those infecting computers with viruses, rather than legitimate users for example patching a bug fix in a program.

4.6.7 Data Protection Act 1984

This Act makes it a criminal offence to hold personal data about living individuals who can be identified (as opposed to, for example, data on an unidentified individual from a questionnaire completed in the street) on computers unless the holder is registered with the Data Protection Registrar. The act does not cover manual files. If the data doesn't relate to individuals, or individuals can't be identified then the act does not apply.

The Act defines data as

> 'Information recorded in a form in which it can be processed automatically in response to instructions given for that purpose'

Processing of data is defined as:

> 'Amending, augmenting, deleting or re-arranging the information'

Individuals are entitled to be supplied with a copy of any information held about them by a registered data holder, although there are exemptions for users such as the police.

Question 4.10

Your lecturer keeps a record of your group of students on his personal computer at home. Is she/he breaking the law? You find a print out of the data for your class in a skip in the college car park. What are the legal implications?

Personal data can only be held for lawful purposes, and there must be security measures in place to prevent unauthorised disclosure of the information.

The Registrar has powers to raid premises and close down businesses which rely on computer systems to ensure compliance with the law. Failure to comply can mean going out of business.

The European Community is also preparing a directive on data security which will allow legal action to be taken against holders of personal information if data is stolen, mislaid or causes damage to an individual.

Question 4.11

You find a copy of your tutors file about you, including a frank appraisal of your attitudes and suitability for employment in the computing industry, left on a table in the college canteen. Has there been a breach of the Data Protection Act?

4.6.8 Summary of legal issues

- Register under the Data Protection Act if applicable

- There is no need to do anything to claim copyright, it is automatic.

- Software designers should ensure that they are not infringing anyone else's copyright.

- Licensing terms should be clearly thought out.

- Employees should clarify who owns copyright in any software they produce, themselves or their employer.

- Deposit a copy of your software with a solicitor or other independent person.

- Clarify if the customer or developer owns copyright in the software.

The contract for the software should cover:

- The specification to meet user requirements.

- The time for development and delivery.

- Whether and to what extent installation and user training are included.

- Future maintenance of the software.

Answer 4.10   *Your lecturer may only store such data if either he/she or the college has registered such usage, and there are appropriate security safeguards in place.*

Answer 4.11   *Not if it was non-computerised data, for example hand-written or typed comments.*

Answer 4.12   *See Section 4.6.8 above.*

- The contract price: fixed or based on time and materials.
- Deposit of source code with a third party in the event of the developer ceasing to trade and the company needing legitimate access to source code.

Question 4.12   Draw up a checklist of legal issues that software developers need to consider when developing systems.

Review questions

1. What are the main standards affecting HCI design?
2. What are the main health and safety issues in HCI design?
3. Summarise the legal issues software designers must consider.

Test questions

1. What is the role of the systems designer in ensuring compliance with EEC 90/270?
2. Draw up a checklist for systems designers to ensure compliance with UK laws on computer systems.
3. Summarise the main issues to be considered when designing systems documentation for users.

5 Systems analysis and the human-computer interface

5.1 Introduction

This chapter considers the different approaches used in systems analysis and design and the way each approaches the issue of interface design, before going on to look at how we can better involve end-users in the design process.

- The software life-cycle and interface design
- Structured methods of systems design
- Data-oriented methods of systems design
- SSADM
- Formal methods
- Iterative design and prototyping
- Human factors in systems design-the HUSAT centre
- Soft systems approaches
- Participative design
- ETHICS
- Multiview
- User software engineering

5.2 The software life-cycle and interface design

Software engineering is concerned with how we should go about the development of software systems. Prior to the 1970s systems development tended to be informal, but the 1970s saw the emergence of structured methods of analysis and design.

The traditional model of the software life-cycle is the waterfall model, made-up of the following stages:

- Requirements specification
- Logical system design
- Physical system design
- Implementation (coding)
- Testing
- Introduction of new system and system maintenance.

In the **waterfall model**, development proceeds from one stage to the next, in a linear progression. Earlier activities are completed before commencement of each successive stage.

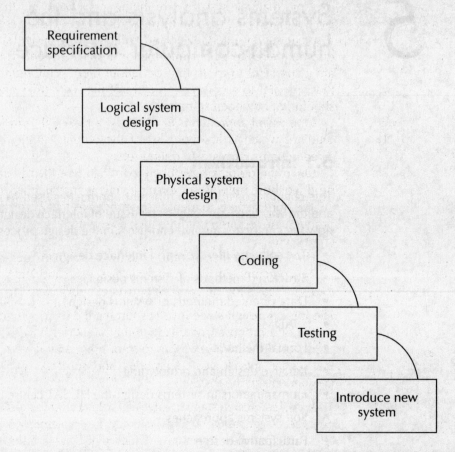

The waterfall model of systems development

5.2.1 Structured methods

In the 1970s the informal approaches to systems design gave way to methods which emphasised structured programming rather than 'spaghetti' code, structured systems design with an emphasis on the processes performed on data, and project management to try and reduce the tendency for systems to go way over budget and schedule.

Approaches included the structured analysis techniques of Gane and Sarson, de Marco, and Jackson Structured Programming / Design (JSD/JSP). It was this era that gave rise to the 'waterfall' model of systems development, where the outputs of one completed stage flowed into the start of the next stage. Tools associated with this period included data flow diagrams (DFDs), structure charts and functional decomposition, whereby processes were broken-down into their components, decision tables and trees, and mini-specifications expressed in pseudocode (a non-language specific form of structured programming).

In the **Requirements specification** stage the designer finds out from the client what the system is intended to do and the context in which it is to work.

This stage is traditionally broken down into problem definition, feasibility study, requirements gathering and requirements analysis. The aim is to describe the desired system and possible implementations of it, together with recommendations.

The skills required of the systems analyst at this stage are the skills of a sociologist, since the analyst needs to obtain complex information about work tasks and environment against a background that is often perceived as threatening to jobs. Where existing manual systems are being computerised, the stage often begins with collecting existing manual forms and documents. The analyst also needs the skills of a social survey interviewer and will probably design structured or semi-structured questionnaires to gather information from the client. The skills of the ethnographer are also useful to try to find out about the taken-for-granted, un-stated assumptions that are vital to a complete picture of the work tasks and environment. These tasks should not be underestimated.

One useful approach is to construct a National Computing Centre (NCC) Systems Outline. which is a simple list of the outputs required from the system-printouts, screen dumps, answers to queries etc.

Once the outputs have been identified, we then identify the inputs necessary to produce those outputs, for example, client and supplier details, product details etc.

The third stage is to identify the processes that must be performed on the inputs to produce the required outputs, such as sorting, extracting records that match specified criteria etc.

Finally, all the files that the system will need are identified.

The outcome of the requirements specification stage is often a document that forms the basis for the contract between the software developer and the client.

The logical design stage involves turning the data from the requirements stage into a model of a proposed new system that identifies how the outputs required are to be produced. This involves some form of functional decomposition (breaking-down) of the system into logical operations and sub-tasks and interrelationships between components of the system.

The physical design stage involves a further refinement of the logical design stage into detailed design of the actual system to be implemented, at a level of detail that will allow programmers to actually write the necessary code. The exact content of screens etc. has to be specified at this stage

The implementation stage is where the physical design specification is turned into actual code, either by writing programs or by the use of program generators and/or CASE (Computer aided software engineering) tools.

The testing stage involves the testing of individual program modules, followed by testing of the complete, integrated application. Prior to testing, a test plan should be constructed containing both typical and abnormal input data. The object of testing is to try to make the program fail in order to expose any problems before it is delivered to the client. Problems will inevitably be more costly to solve after delivery.

On completion of testing, the system is ready for **hand-over to the client**. This stage will normally involve training of users on the new system, followed by any necessary system maintenance.

5.2.2 Summary of the traditional waterfall approach

- The approach is linear, regarding stages as occurring in sequence.

- The stages are clear-cut, allowing better project management.

- It is assumed that all the requirements are known before actual design commences.

Question 5.1   What are the most important features of the waterfall model?

5.2.3 Problems with the approach

In practice, requirements often change as the project progresses.

It has been estimated that around 30-40% of computer projects are massively over budget, over time and fail to do the job they were supposed to do. Of the remainder, around half deliver at best only marginal benefits. It has been found that the single major source of errors is the requirements stage, where almost 60% of errors occur, followed by the design stage, with around 25%, and coding responsible for 7%. Current design practice is to devote the majority of time to the physical design, coding and testing stages, responsible for around 60% of time, with only around 10% devoted to requirements gathering and 15% to logical design. The conclusion from these figures seems to be that most errors occur in the earliest stages of the life-cycle (around 85% of errors in the first two stages) yet only around 25% of time and resources are devoted to these areas.

In the 1970s it was assumed that most systems design involved the replacement of manual systems with computerised systems, a reasonable assumption at the time. Structured methods of analysis therefore assumed that the requirements of the new system were simply those of the old system, with the emphasis being placed on turning the manual system into a correct computerised implementation, and avoiding the cost and time over-runs that had become typical of large-scale systems development. However, as we have seen from the above, later evidence showed that it was at the requirements stage that most errors were made.

From the point of view of interface design, structured analysis has little or nothing to say, since in this period systems were always large-scale and text based, with no possibilities of direct manipulation graphical user interfaces. Hardware resources were also seen as expensive and scarce, with emphasis being placed on most efficient code design.

Question 5.2   Why was little attention paid to interface issues in the 1970s?

5.2.4 Alternative approaches to systems design

The above figures for systems failure demonstrate clearly the need to find acceptable alternative approaches.

5.2.5 Data-oriented methods

In the 1980s there emerged a growing need for new types of systems which didn't exist as manual systems, such as management information systems (MIS) and decision-support systems (DSS). The requirements for such systems were less well understood than traditional data processing systems, so methods which paid more attention to the requirements gathering stage had to be developed. Fundamentally, what was required was a better understanding of requirements. Conceptual modelling techniques such as Entity-Relationship modelling (E-R) attempted to capture details of the conceptual entities that were needed in the new systems. Approaches associated with this period include Information engineering and SSADM (Structured Systems Analysis and Design Methodology), the official UK government systems development methodology.

5.2.6 SSADM

The stages of SSADM are as follows:

Stage 0   Feasibility Study. This is a shortened high-level version of the requirements analysis and specification stages, concluding with an evaluation of different system options and an assessment of the feasibility of the project.

Stage 1 & 2 Requirements Analysis. Stage 1 investigates the current environment, identifying problems and improvements that can be made. Users of the proposed system are also identified. Physical DFDs are produced for current data processing activities, which are then transformed into logical DFDs. The logical data structure is modelled using E-R diagrams.

Stage 2   Three to six business system options are presented which describe proposed information systems and how they meet both functional requirements and non-functional requirements such as impact of the proposed system on the organisation, volumes of data, costs and timings etc. System boundaries are established at this stage.

Stage 3   Requirements specification. A detailed specification is produced using the chosen business system option from stage 2. The DFDs and E-Rs are modified to match the selected business system option and non-functional requirements are defined. Functions are identified from DFDs and JSP (Jackson Structured Programming) diagrams constructed to show the structure of input and output. Entity Life Histories (ELHs) are constructed to show the effects of time on entities.

Stages 4 & 5 Logical System Specification. Stage 4 is the Technical System Options stage, where different technical ways of meeting the specification are assessed to find the best option. Stage 5 is the Logical Design stage, where attention is focused on the interface design. Entity modelling is used for logical database design and to identify enquiry and update processes. Dialogue features such as menu structures and commands are designed.

Stage 6   Physical Design. This is the actual implementation of the design using 4GLs, packages or a programming language.

SSADM Version 4: Summary

Stage 0	Feasibility	010	Prepare for feasibility study
		020	Define the problem
		030	Select feasibility option
		040	Assemble feasibility report
Stage 1	Investigation	110	Establish analysis framework
	of current	120	Investigate & define requirements
	environment	130	investigate current processing
		140	Investigate current data
		150	Derive logical view of current services
		160	Assemble investigation results

Answer 5.1   *The idea that each earlier stage is complete before moving to the next stage. Since testing only occurs towards the end of the life-cycle, feedback from end-users isn't obtained until it is really too late to change the design.*

Answer 5.2   *Computerisation at this time was simply seen as the replacement of human tasks with computer tasks, so requirements were seen as unproblematic. The cost and technological limitations of hardware meant that there was no question of considering graphics-based interfaces, and most users were trained staff rather than the typical end-user of today.*

Stage 2	Business system options	210 220	Define business system options Select business system options
Stage 3	Definition of requirements	310 320 330 340 350 360 370 380	Define required system processing Develop required data model Derive system functions Enhance required data model Prototype I/O interfaces Develop processing specification Confirm system objectives Assemble requirements specification
Stage 4	Technical system options	410 420	Define technical system options Select technical system options
Stage 5	Logical design	510 520 530 540	Define user dialogues Define update processing Define enquiry processing Assemble logical design
Stage 6	Physical design	610 620 630 640 650 660 670	Prepare for physical design Create physical data design Create function component implementation map Optimise physical data design Complete function specification Consolidate process data interface Assemble physical design

5.2.7 Interface design in SSADM Version 4

SSADM is seen as a set of guidelines rather than rigid rules for system development. For example, step 420 involves the use of application style guides if they exist, rather than prescribing a particular dialogue style. One of the major differences between versions 3 and 4 of SSADM is the incorporation of interface design stages in version 4. A central feature of version 4 is the user-based view of system functions, with processing structures built around these user views. SSADM Functions are derived from the services and facilities which system users wish to see grouped together in meaningful clusters. Functions combine data flows with processes in order to provide the facilities required, for example, to issue a book in a computerised library system involves data flows such as book and borrower details, together with processes such as checking the borrower's record for overdue books and fines etc.

The main dialogue design stages in SSADM are stages 420, where application style guides are selected or created, 510 where the actual dialogue is designed, and 350, the optional prototyping stage, where the dialogues are tested with end-users and the design modified if required. It is interesting to note that the prototyping stage occurs before the dialogue design stage, an indication of the origins of SSADM in earlier design methodologies where dialogue design was seen as something that could be bolted on to a more-or-less completed system design.

Question 5.3   How does SSADM version 4 differ from the waterfall model described earlier?

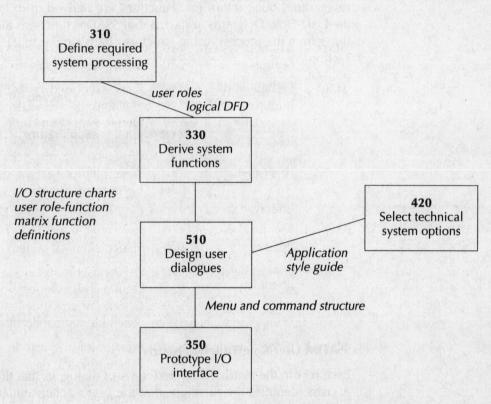

Summary of Interface design stages in SSADM version 4

The user roles are identified in stage 310 and a user role table is constructed to show the role, the job title and the main job activities, as in the example below. The table is derived from the user catalogue, which is simply a list of users of the information system and their activities.

User role	Job title	Activities
reserver	main library counter worker	reserve book
book finder	main library counter worker	locate book in catalogue
	borrower	

Answer 5.3

SSADM introduces the idea of iterative design, through the use of a cycle of design-prototype-re-design. It also pays more attention to the requirements analysis and interface design stages.

User role table

From the user roles table a User Role/Function matrix is constructed which plots user roles against functions, which are groups of related activities such as book issue, book reservation, book return etc. Functions are derived from the processes identified in the Data Flow Diagrams in stage 3, but SSADM functions also show input and output flows from the process, using Structure charts similar to JSP structure charts (see later section).

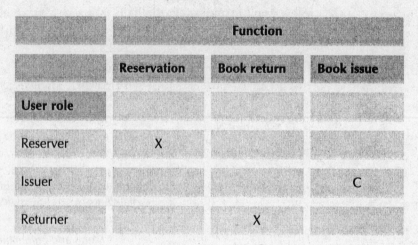

	Function		
	Reservation	Book return	Book issue
User role			
Reserver	X		
Issuer			C
Returner		X	

SSADM User Role/Function Matrix

SSADM User Role/Function Matrix

Each row in the matrix identifies the set of dialogues that the user requires access to. A cross identifies the functions that the user's action initiates. A C is used to show 'critical' dialogues, i.e. those with demanding performance requirements in terms of speed, accuracy etc.

The **Function Definitions** are text-based descriptions of functions such as book reservation, together with details of associated inputs, outputs, error handling and user roles.

The input/output structure charts, user role/function matrix, function definitions together with any relevant application style guide (such as the Apple style guide etc.) are used in stage 510 to design the actual menus, commands and other interface features, which are then tested on end-users (and test results logged) in the proto-typing stage. Several iterations of the dialogue design and prototyping stages are normally necessary before acceptance criteria are met, at which stage the final dialogue design forms the output to the Assemble Logical Design stage 540.

While SSADM 4 clearly acknowledges the importance of interface design and testing, it provides very little guidance on *how* interface design should actually occur as opposed to *when* it occurs. As a result, SSADM cannot be thought of as an interface design method.

Question 5.4

How does SSADM show the screen dialogues that the end user will need?

5.2.8 Formal methods of design

One of the problems with traditional approaches to systems design is that of *proving* that the system will work. Formal methods address this problem by attempting to show that a program works exactly according to its specification, known as verification. The specification is produced at the design stage, in a language with a precisely defined syntax such as predicate logic or Z, or a sub-set of a programming language such as C or Pascal. While such approaches can lead to the production of a specification using the appropriate formalism at the design stage, which can be used to verify that the resulting program is consistent with the specification; we have seen in the last section that the majority of errors occur before the design stage. Formal methods can help turn specifications into verifiable code, but they don't solve the problems of inadequate requirements analysis and specification.

Question 5.5

Why don't formal methods help in the design of interfaces?

5.2.9 Iterative design and prototyping

The iterative approach to systems design involves going back to previous stages a number of times, rather than the rigid, sequenced progression from one stage to the next of the waterfall model. Iteration recognises that as we go through the life-cycle stages we are likely to discover information that requires us to revise the assumptions made in previous stages. The only way we can be really certain about an interface is to build it and test it out on some typical users. The design can then be modified in the light of our tests. However, we clearly can't build a complete system first then test it, hence the need to iteratively cycle through each stage several times.

Prototypes are models of the system that implement a limited range of the systems features and functions, for example we could design an opening screen with menus and ask users to evaluate the screen design without our prototype screen actually doing anything. A prototype can be anything from a pencil and paper sketch of a screen to a cut-down version of the final product.

Prototypes can be throw-away, where the prototype is tested but then discarded, or it can be evolutionary, where it is retained as the basis for the next interface design. However, it is important to realise that not all aspects of usability can be assessed from prototypes. In particular, they can't be used to assess features such as task performance times and reliability. Nevertheless, they can provide important usability feedback at the design stage, as has been demonstrated by Molich and Nielsen's 'Discount Usability Engineering' approach to interface design (see Chapter 6).

Question 5.6

Why do we use prototypes, and what are they?

Types of prototyping

Storyboards are screen designs without any actual functionality, they are non-working screens that can be evaluated by users in terms of features such as language, screen messages, screen layout and use of colour etc. They can be produced either with graphics packages, or with screen or forms design packages such as the screen design options available in Access and Visual Basic.

A set of such non-functioning screen designs can be animated to provide an idea of the sequence of screens displayed to the user by using animation facilities to link the screens, for example the slide show features of packages such as Excel, Micrografix Designer, Lotus Freelance and Multimedia Toolbook.

Answer 5.4	*See the above section for details of the user role/function matrix.*
Answer 5.5	*Because they are only concerned with proving that a program correctly implements a given specification, using mathematical and logic techniques. However, whether or not the specification adequately captures the user requirements is a human problem that can't be subjected to the same kind of formal techniques of analysis.*
Answer 5.6	*See the section above. They are limited-functionality mock-ups of interface designs, using anything from pencil and paper sketches to visual basic forms.*

Limited-functionality prototypes allow some of the interactive nature of the interface to be incorporated and tested, without the need to build complete systems. Event-driven programming environments such as Visual Basic and HyperCard make the production of such prototypes very quick.

Wizard of Oz prototyping is where the missing functionality of the prototype is provided by one of the designers translating user inputs into commands that will work on the prototype. The user is not aware of the designers presence, and to all intents and purposes believes that he or she is using a fully functioning system.

Prototyping is an essential component of iterative design, but it can't solve all of the problems of traditional design methods. In particular, prototyping can't adequately evaluate aspects of usability such as task performance. However, it is an important way of involving end-users in interface design at the earliest stages.

5.3 Human factors in Information Systems Design: the work of the HUSAT Centre at Loughborough University

The recognition during the 1980s of the failures of structured analysis and design techniques lead to the establishment of the above research centre, with a brief to find ways of incorporating human factors into systems analysis and design.

5.3.1 DIADEM

The Departmental Integrated Application Development Methodology (DIADEM) aimed to include human factors in SSADM version 3. It identified the following human factors extensions:

1. User analysis
2. User participation in decision-making
3. User participation in acceptance criteria
4. Methods of user involvement
5. Job design
6. Task allocation
7. User support
8. Human-computer interface design

9.   Prototyping

10.   Workstation design

11.   Management of change

12.   Consideration of the impact of systems on the organisation

The DIADEM team identified ways of improving SSADM in each of the above areas that could be taught to systems developers, resulting in a set of manuals covering the areas. The emphasis was on teaching traditional analysts the necessary human factors skills, and in involving users more at the requirements specification stage of design, where most errors are traditionally made. However, the highly structured and sequential nature of SSADM with its adherence to a traditional 'waterfall' model of systems development made it difficult to incorporate such an iterative approach. some features of the approach appear in other methods such as the ETHICS approach (see below).

5.3.2 HUFIT

The Human Factors in Information Technology (HUFIT) project was concerned with promoting the adoption by systems developers of a user-centred design approach, through the development of a set of teachable techniques covering the following areas:

1.   User mapping: the 'fit' between users' conceptual models and system goals

2.   User and task characteristics affecting systems

3.   Usability specifications that can be objectively measured using metrics (see Chapter 8)

4.   User requirements summary

5.   Functionality matrix identifying user, task and environmental characteristics and priorities

6.   Human-computer interface design.

5.3.3 Human Factors Guidelines

The third method from HUSAT was designed to deal with real-time systems development for the UK Ministry of Defence. They focus on the early stages of development, especially the Requirements Specification stage, where Stakeholders, Tasks, and the identification of the human-computer boundary and allocation of tasks to people or computers are considered.

Overall, the HUSAT approach emphasises the integration of human factors in systems design methods, but in a way which simply seeks to obtain better quality and more realistic information about user tasks and performance than more traditional methods. This is in contrast to some of the more participative design methods such as the 'Scandinavian school'. Bjorn-Anderson has made the point that the human factors approach seems to aim to make minor adjustments in order to improve measures of systems productivity, rather than to genuinely challenge existing organisational and work patterns.

Question 5.7   What are the limitations of the HUSAT approach?

Answer 5.7

There is no attempt to take account of all users interests in the way that the ETHICS and 'Scandinavian' approaches to systems design do. Rather the focus is on manipulating human factors to enhance productivity.

5.4 Soft Systems Methodology (SSM)

SSM is not a systems design method, rather it is concerned with identifying broader human issues that need to be taken into account by systems designers. It originates from the work of Checkland in the early 1980s, and has been incorporated into the COMPACT and MULTIVIEW systems design methods (see below).

Stages of SSM

Stages 1 & 2: The problem situation

Building a 'rich picture' of the problem situation. The rich picture is constructed by listing as many people, organisations etc. as are involved in or influence the system. Who has a stake in the system, and what are their perceptions and ability to influence the system? A variety of perspectives on the problem situation should be identified.

Stage 3: Root definition

The root definition tries to describe in one sentence the important aspects of the system. The completeness of the root definition is assessed by performing a CATWOE test:

  Customers of the system
  Actors who perform the activities of the system
  Transformations-the actual activities that occur within the system
  Weltanshauung – the perspective or viewpoint expressed in the root definition
  Owner of the system
  Environment in which the system operates

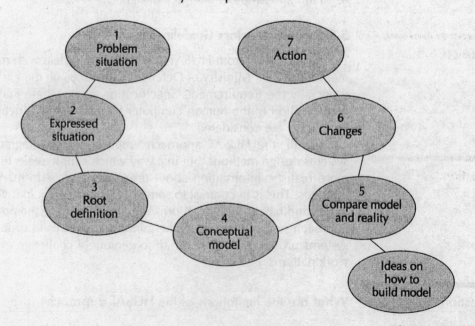

The stages of SSM

An example of a root definition for a university library could be:

> 'A system to lend appropriate books to students and staff of the university, through the library staff, operating on the university campus, owned and funded by the university and to keep appropriate records of lending and book purchasing transactions so as to meet financial controls stipulated by the government, university and higher education funding council'.

Note that there is more than one possible root definition for any system. The deliberate aim is to get designers to think about all the possible stakeholders in the system.

Stage 4: Conceptual Model

The Conceptual model describes what a system would need to do so that its existence would be the root definition in stage 3. It should contain verbs describing processes concerned with the system's purpose, performance, decision-making, resources, and environment. It may describe several levels of analysis. Data Flow Diagrams could be used to build conceptual models, since they focus on the processes that the system could perform.

Stage 5: Compare model with reality

This stage is based around a discussion of the differences between the two, and possible new systems models. This may result in a deepening of the rich picture and a return to stage 3 and another iteration of the cycle. Alternatively, there may be sufficient agreement to move to stage 6.

Stage 6 & 7: Change and action

Stage 6 involves the clarification of the ideas for change into a new systems design, followed by the implementation of that design. These stages can make use of the techniques of structured systems analysis, such as those of SSADM, since once stage 5 is completed SSM doesn't differ fundamentally from structured approaches, other than its emphasis on the use of prototyping.

In summary, SSM is more a method to think about the issues involved in systems analysis and design than a set of tools for the systems designer. However, its insights have been incorporated into design frameworks such as Multiview and Compact.

Question 5.8

It takes practice to use SSM. Try the following exercises, remembering that there is no 'right' answer to them.

Construct a root definition and perform a CATWOE test on a college or university student registration system and on an order processing system for a mail order retailer.

Question 5.9

Which of the traditional stages of systems analysis and design does SSM focus on?

5.5 COMPACT

Compact was developed by the UK civil service for small office systems development, defined as single-site projects costing less than £100,000 and lasting three to four months.

Answer 5.8

For example, 'A system to enrol bona-fide students into the college in line with agreed procedures of the college and the appropriate funding body and to keep accurate, up to date records to meet the needs of the staff.' There are no hard and fast correct answers.

Answer 5.9

SSM focuses on the identification and representation of the different groups involved and their perceptions and requirements, which may conflict with each other. So it is mainly concerned with the requirements analysis stages of design.

It is based on Soft Systems Methodology and emphasises the participation of users, the organisational structure of the office, and analysis rather than design. It uses techniques designed to allow users to raise and interpret issues which they feel are relevant, rather than confining itself to data processing issues.

Compact uses SSM to analyse problems, and Data Flow Diagrams for designing the business solution on the grounds that DFDs are easy to draw and interpret for end-users. It contains four stages and fifteen steps, each of which is broken down into a total of 44 tasks.

Stage 1: Initiation

Step 1   Project Brief: an investigation of what the project aims are and how they might be achieved

Stage 2: Study

Step 2   Function Analysis: this is the core of COMPACT and uses SSM to describe the required systems activities in terms of root definitions which are then refined into an Agreed Activity Model (AAM).

Step 3   Organisation Analysis: this stage analyses what currently happens and compares it to the AAM, similar to stage 5 in SSM

Step 4   Information Analysis: similar to stage 3, but with the emphasis on analysis of information. DFDs can be used here.

Step 5   Business Requirements: this identifies alternative proposals which are subjected to a cost-benefit analysis and presented as a set of alternatives to the project board.

Step 6   Business solutions: here a logical model of the proposed solution is developed and agreed using DFDs.

Step 7   Technical Options: this stage identifies alternative technical solutions which are presented to the project board for selection.

Step 8   Organisational Option: this is a crucial step since it is concerned with social aspects of the work with the aim of ensuring participation, efficiency, effectiveness and work satisfaction, all of which are important components of systems usability. It involves the setting of social objectives (in much the same way as the ETHICS socio-technical approach to systems design) and the selection of an organisational option from alternatives.

Stage 3: Development and Implementation

Step 9   Procurement: the ordering, delivery, installation and acceptance of equipment.

Step 10   Office Design and Preparation: physical office design

Step 11   Organisation Design: this step is concerned with the design of work procedures and job descriptions and gradings. it is based around the DFDs from step 6.

Step 12   System Development: this is the step where the user interface is defined and documentation is produced. It is important to match systems to user conceptual models, rather than trying to fit users to the system. Usability issues are crucial at this step.

Step 13   Training: the planning and delivery of training

Step 14   Handover and acceptance

Stage 4   Business Support

Step 15   Business Support: concerned with ongoing support that the system may require.

In conclusion, COMPACT attempts to combine the insights of SSM with the structured approach of SSADM in the development of small office systems. Note that it uses Data Flow Diagrams as its main analysis and design tool throughout.

5.6 Participative design

We have seen above that most computer systems fail to deliver the expected benefits, with estimates as high as 80% of systems either not working or delivering at best marginal benefits. Research has shown that over half of failures are due to incomplete requirements analysis, and a further quarter occur in the design stage.

Typically, projects are initiated at board level in organisations, and are imposed on end-users with little or no consultation. However, the senior managers responsible for initiating change are not usually end-users of the systems. *Participative* approaches to system design acknowledge the following factors:

- that the system has to be designed to meet the requirements of the actual users of the system, rather than the system 'owners'.

- that the introduction of new systems is in itself likely to change the informal relationships within the organisation, for example a system that allows some workers to 'telecommute' by working from home may be seen by supervisors as diminishing their power.

- that it is only after completion of initial design work and the prototyping of interfaces with end-users that a more or less complete description of user requirements is possible.

Some participative approaches go even further, and take the view that users have the right to be involved in the design of work systems. Such a view is associated with the 'Scandinavian' approach to systems design. In the Scandinavian countries it is acknowledged that there may be conflicts of interests between workers and managers, and information systems are not seen as neutral. Systems design concentrates on identifying and clearly defining the viewpoints of the different groups and ensuring that their views are represented. In the Scandinavian countries, this representational role is usually taken on by the trade unions, who have close links with research organisations. Like the Soft-systems, Multiview (see section 5.8) and Sociotechnical approaches, the Scandinavian approach sets out to make sure that all relevant viewpoints are made visible. Unlike the other approaches mentioned here it places less emphasis on resolving the conflicts. In practice, such approaches might work like ETHICS, with separate teams of developers each representing the significant interest groups. Where decisions have to made between competing prototypes, these can be made by negotiation or referral to some other body, without necessarily assuming that all conflicts need to be resolved before systems development can continue.

In summary, participative approaches emphasise an early focus on user involvement and feedback, user involvement in design, and iterative design-prototyping-feedback-design cycles. They also usually aim to improve the work environment and employee task satisfaction. Below we look at some participative design methods in more detail.

Question 5.10   Briefly summarise the main characteristics of Participative approaches.

5.7 ETHICS

Ethics stands for Effective Technical and Human Implementation of Computer Systems. It is based on a socio-technical approach to systems development which regards participation by users and potential users not simply as part of the requirements gathering process, but as a right in itself.

Ethics identifies two parallel strands of systems development; the technical and the social, with separate design teams being established for each strand. There is a focus on user satisfaction that fits in well with current definitions of software usability such as those emerging from ISO 9241.

In stage 6, the final stage, a detailed list of tasks is compiled and checked for job satisfaction. If the highest ranked technical solution from stage 5 scores well it is adopted, otherwise the next solution is tried and so on.

ETHICS is a truly participatory approach in that the goals of users as well as task goals are considered by two separate specialist design teams, who then choose from a range of possible solutions by reference to pre-determined criteria. Where one proposed solution ranks highest on both technical and social criteria, it is adopted. Otherwise, alternative solutions are examined.

Summary of the stages of ETHICS

Stage 1: Systems analysis
ETHICS is similar to other systems development approaches in the initial steps of this stage. However it then identifies two sets of goals, *task* and *satisfaction* goals, which are then ranked by all participants on a 5-point scale.

1. Identify problem
2. Identify system boundaries
3. Describe existing system
4. Specify key objectives
5. Identify key tasks
6. Identify sets of tasks

	7. Identify information needs
	8. Identify variance
	9. Diagnose job satisfaction needs
	10. Forecast future needs
	11. Set and rank efficiency and job satisfaction needs
	12. Identify technical and business constraints
Stage 2: Socio-technical systems design Two groups are formed, one focusing on the technical side, the other on the social. The objectives from Stage 1 are set out in order of priority and checked for compatibility before the technical and social decisions are taken.	13. Identify social constraints 14. Identify technical resources available 15. Identify social resources available 16. Specify priority technical and business objectives 17. Specify priority social objectives 18. Check social and technical objectives for compatibility 19. Take technical decisions 20. Take social decisions
Stage 3: Set out alternative solutions These are evaluated against the criteria of priority, constraints, and resources. A short list of possible solutions is then drawn up.	21. Set out alternative technical solutions 22. Set out alternative social solutions
Stage 4 This merges solutions from Stage 3 to see which are most compatible.	23. Set out compatible socio-technical solutions
Stage 5 The results of Stage 4 are ranked using criteria from 3.	24. Rank compatible pairs of socio-technical solutions
Stage 6: Detailed design	25. Prepare detailed design work

5.8 Multiview

Multiview is based on Soft Systems Methodology and has the following five stages:

1. Analysis of human activity
2. Analysis of information
3. Analysis and design of socio-technical aspects
4. Design of the human-computer interface
5. Design of technical aspects

Participative approaches are user-centred, recognising that all too often the main contact is between systems analysts and board members, or marketing departments and board members, rather than contact with actual end-users and their participation in design teams.

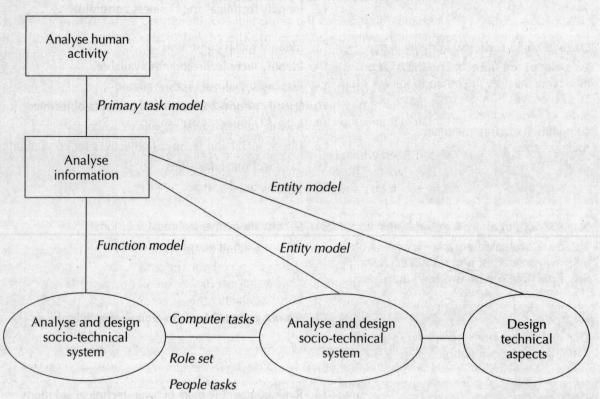

Stages of Multiview

Multiview is both task and issue-related, and as its name suggests, tries to take account of multiple views of the system and its users.

Multiview's design stages (3-5) produce the following outputs and issues:

Output	Issues
Social aspects	How will it affect me?
Role-set	Will jobs change? In what ways?
People tasks	What will users have to do?
Human-Computer interface	How will users work with the computer? What inputs and outputs are there?
Database	What data are involved?
Database Maintenance	How will data integrity be maintained?
Recovery	What happens when the system goes wrong?
Monitoring	Is the system performing to specification?
Control	How are security and error-detection dealt with?

Information retrieval	What information can be obtained from the system?
Application	What will the system do?
Inputs and outputs for non-application areas	Will it affect anything else on the computer sub-system?

5.8.1 Stage 1: Analyse human activity

Multiview emphasises the importance of identifying and debating issues in stage 1, which is heavily based on SSM. The central focus of stage 1 is on identifying the world-view (or views) or Weltaunschauung that will form the basis for describing system requirements.

Like SSM, Multiview creates a 'rich picture' of the problem situation from which themes emerge, which in turn are used to generate a root definition of the system which is then subjected to a CATWOE test (see section on SSM above).

When an agreed root definition emerges a conceptual model of the system is constructed which is then compared to reality, with differences and possible changes being debated by the design team until an agreed conceptual model is arrived at which can be carried forward to stage 2.

5.8.2 Stage 2-Analysis of Information

This stage is concerned with identifying the functions and entities of the system.

The main function of the system is identified and further broken-down into sub-functions until the analyst feels that no further break-down is necessary. Such functional decomposition is very similar to the approach taken in Jackson Structured Programming (JSP), where the function breakdown is shown in the form of function charts.

Data flow diagrams are then produced to show the sequence of system events. DFDs and function charts from this stage then form the inputs to stage 3.

The entity model is constructed using Entity-Relationship diagrams, and forms the input to stages 4 and 5.

5.8.3 Stage 3: Analysis and Design of the Socio-technical aspects

This stage is based on Mumford's ETHICS approach, discussed above. The stage involves the separate identification of possible technical and social systems and their matching and ranking, with the aim of selecting the best of the possible systems, which will then determine the people tasks, computer tasks, role-set and social aspects of the system.

5.8.4 Stage 4: Design of the Human-Computer Interface

The inputs to stage 4 are the entity models from stage 2, and the people tasks, computer tasks and role-sets from stage 3. The concern at this stage is firstly to identify batch-processing and on-line tasks, and then to consider the dialogues between user and computer. The technical requirements to fulfil the required interface are then output to stage 5.

5.8.5 Stage 5: Design of the Technical Aspects

Inputs to the stage are the entity model from stage 2 and technical requirements from stage 4. Since human issues have already been considered, this stage concentrates on technical implementation issues. The major outputs are the application database, along with maintenance, control, recovery and monitoring aspects of the system.

While Multiview combines techniques such as DFDs with Soft systems and ETHICS approaches, it is very sketchy on detailed human-computer interface design issues, providing little clear guidance for designers.

Question 5.11

Make a chart comparing Multiview and ETHICS, identifying similarities and differences between the two approaches.

5.9 Jackson Structured Programming/Design (JSP/JSD)

JSP is a data-oriented approach to systems design, based on top-down functional decomposition which simply means that the designer starts with the broad task (for example, design an employee record system) which is then broken-down into its components.

JSP involves the following steps:

1. Define the structure of the data

2. Identify the main processing tasks to be performed on the data

3. Define the program structure from step 2 above

4. Break-down the processing tasks (decompose them) into single programming steps

JSP starts by breaking-down the processing problem into its component tasks, for example an employee record system could be broken down into the following operations that end-users typically perform:

1. Add new employee record

2. Delete employee record

3. Amend employee record

4. Print employee record

5. Print summary report of selected employee information, for example details of all employees over the age of 55 etc.

Each task is then further broken down into ever smaller parts until you can't simplify any further. The resulting breakdown is shown in a tree diagram such as the one below:

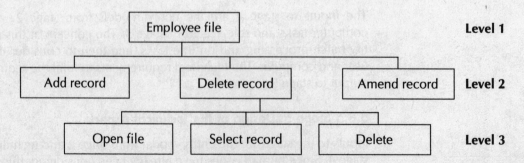

Example of a JSP Diagram Chart for an employee file

JSP was designed to allow the development of structured programs, but its JSD notation can be used to represent the decomposition of tasks into sub-tasks in a notation that is likely to be familiar with systems designers who are not HCI experts. It is therefore a useful tool for task analysis. JSD diagrams can be used to represent the structure of menus in an interface in a way which is easily understandable and which shows the hierarchy of menus.

Question 5.12

Use JSP to decompose and represent the following tasks:

1. The process of applying for a place at college.
2. The process of shopping for goods at a catalogue store similar to Argos.

5.10 User Software Engineering (USE)

USE was devised in the mid-1980s by Wasserman, and has as its aim the production of systems that meet users' requirements in terms of functionality, are easy to use, and can easily be adapted to changes in user needs. As a method it also aims to raise developers' productivity through automating the production of systems using PLAIN, a programming language. Early involvement of end-users and the design and testing of working prototypes are major characteristics of USE.

Stages of USE:

1. Requirements analysis
2. Design user interface
3. Prototype interface
4. Build functional prototype

Detailed steps:

1. Requirements analysis: data and activity modelling and identification of user characteristics
2. Design of partially-functional prototype dialogues and interfaces
3. User testing of prototype interface
4. Completion of the full functional specification of the system using narrative text.
5. Preliminary relational database design.
6. Creation of a functional prototype system, providing at least some, possibly all, of the system's functions.
7. Formal specification of the system operations
8. System design at the architectural and module levels.
9. Implementation in PLAIN
11. Testing.

USE was an early attempt to automate the interface design process. However, its use of state transition diagrams to represent the interface is really only suitable for the text-based dialogue styles available in the mid-1980s, rather than the graphical user interfaces common in the 1990s. It is rather vague on issues of usability measurement, not surprising given its origins in the 1980s.

Answer 5.11

Both seek to investigate alternative views of the problem situation, however ETHICS treats the requirements stage as less problematic than Multiview. Neither approach provide any detailed guidance on interface design.

Answer 5.12

Again, there is no 'correct' answer. A possible solution would be:

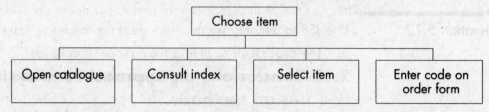

Since the appearance of the USE method, others have tried to improve it using methods based on entity-relationship models which are then input to expert systems, such as the GENIUS system. However, the rule-base in GENIUS is itself based on the Smith and Mosier Guidelines (see below) which date from 1986 and although comprehensive (there are 944 separate guidelines), date from an era of text-based rather than GUI interfaces so are limited in their applicability to modern systems development. Whilst initially a promising looking approach to the automation of interface design, USE has so far failed to live up to that promise. In its attempt to use formal methods to specify interfaces it was largely ignoring the problems of different user views that soft systems approaches try to deal with.

5.11 The Star Model of the system life-cycle

Most approaches to systems design still use a 'stage' model, albeit with the addition of iteration and prototyping in the later methods such as Multiview. However, the star model is based on the principle that systems analysis and design can start at any stage and doesn't have to follow a particular logical progression. The model is based on studies of how systems are actually designed in practice, with development proceeding simultaneously in both a top-down and bottom-up fashion.

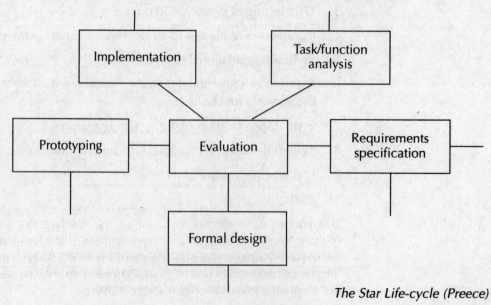

The Star Life-cycle (Preece)

In the star life-cycle, development may begin at any 'stage'. The approach emphasises rapid prototyping and alternating bottom-up and top-down design approaches. Evaluation is placed at the centre of the model, to emphasise its importance, compared with the testing stage in traditional design methods. The model can utilise a variety of support tools, from informal sketches and diagrams to formal notations, checklists, style guides and guidelines. As a representation of how designers actually go about the process of design, it is very useful, but doesn't provide detailed techniques for interface design.

5.12 Conclusions on approaches to systems analysis and design methods.

As we have seen above, there is no one method that satisfactorily allows us to design systems interfaces. Most methods described have their strengths, but none are complete. The later methods described which combine soft systems approaches to the requirements analysis problem with participation by end users and the use of prototyping and iterative design offer the most scope for the design of usable effective systems, but tend to lack detail as to just how to design interfaces.

Question 5.13

Draw up a chart listing the strengths and weaknesses of each of the methods of analysis and design dealt with in this chapter. Try to rate them on a scale of 1 (not very useful) to 7 (very useful) for how useful they are to systems design.

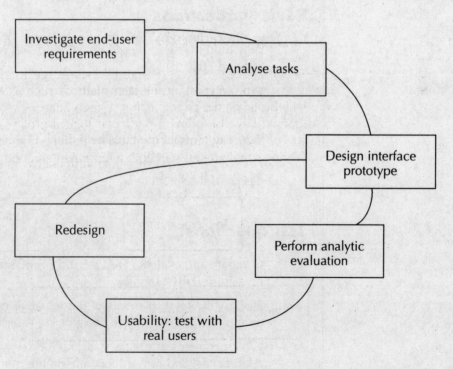

A proposed systems life-cycle for systems interface design

In the above model, design is user-centred, iterative and relies in usability testing with real users. The model is compatible with the star life cycle model discussed earlier, in that the process can be entered at many points, although in practice one is likely to start with an analysis of user requirements.

Answer 5.13

Method	Strengths	Weaknesses
SSADM	Clear procedures	Lacks detailed I/F design
Formal Methods	Can prove that code meets specification	Ignores problems at requirements stage
Iterative design	Uses feedback from user	Not a method so much as an approach
SSM	Concentrates on defining the problem	Lacks detailed design stages
Compact	Combines SSM with traditional tools	Lacks detail on I/F design
Participative Design	Acknowledges inherent conflicts at work	Lacks detail on I/F design
Ethics	Considers social as well as technical issues	Lacks detail on I/F design
Multiview	Combines SSM with structured methods	Lacks detail on I/F design
JSP/JSD	Good for task decomposition	Weak on problem definition and I/F design
USE	Attempts to automate design	Not suited to modern GUIs

Review questions

1. Why didn't systems designers bother much with interface design in the 60s and 70s?

2. Why do most large systems fail?

3. What is SSADM and how well does it support interface design?

4. Why can't formal methods help much in interface design?

5. How do soft systems and participative design approaches help the design of the interface?

Test questions

1. Compare and evaluate SSADM and ETHICS as approaches to the design of user-friendly systems.

2. Discuss the relative merits of participative design and formal methods as approaches to interface design.

3. What problems are there with traditional systems analysis and design approaches, and how adequately do the more user-centred approaches overcome them?

6 Designing interfaces

Introduction

This chapter looks at practical tools and methods for the analysis of user activities and design of interfaces.

- Task Analysis
- Conceptual Modelling
- Organisational Factors
- Guidelines, Style Guides and Heuristics
- Tools for Interface Design

6.1 Task analysis

We now turn from the methods used for systems analysis and design to a consideration of some of the more detailed approaches to the analysis of user tasks.

Task analysis is concerned with analysing *what* people do when going about their work, in terms of the way that tasks are broken-down or decomposed into sub-tasks, for example, doing the washing can be broken down into collecting the dirty washing, loading it into the washing machine, loading the powder and fabric conditioner, setting the machine, switching it on, emptying it and hanging the washing out. Task analysis is also interested in what knowledge users need in order to perform their tasks, and in the objects, actors and actions that are performed during the task.

Task analysis is concerned with the *observation* of existing systems and the recording of tasks. However, since much software development is concerned with replacing existing systems, it is a useful part of the requirements capture stage of systems analysis.

Unlike cognitive models of users such as GOMS, task analysis is largely concerned with observable behaviour of relevant actors. GOMS in contrast attempts to construct an internal mental representation of tasks (see Chapter 7 for a fuller account of GOMS).

Task decomposition can take the form of a narrative account, such as the example above, but it is often preferable to use JSD-like diagrams to represent tasks and sub-tasks. The example above could be represented as follows:

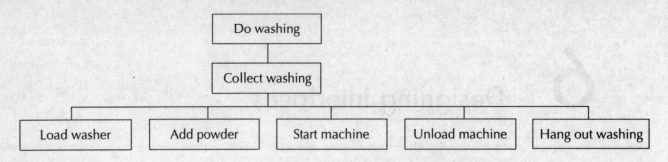

Outline Hierarchical Task Analysis (HTA) diagram for doing the washing

With task analysis, there is no single right answer. The diagrams or narratives produced are checked with end-users and other members of the design team, possibly using 'walkthrough' techniques (see Chapter 8) to ensure that all relevant sub-tasks are included.

Question 6.1

In what ways does task analysis differ from GOMS?

A further use of task analysis is in the design of manuals and training courses. For example, a manual could take one level of an HTA diagram such as the above as the basis for a chapter, with one page being devoted to the decomposed tasks. Where a system is being upgraded or replaced, a task analysis can be performed for old and new systems and a comparison of the two HTA diagrams will reveal areas to include in the training course.

Knowledge-based task analysis techniques such as Task Analysis for Knowledge Description (TAKD) list all the objects and actions involved in the task. In one approach, each item is placed on a card and groups of end-users are asked to sort them into related items. In this way the designer obtains the user's view of task structures. Where there are different groups of user, different classifications are likely to emerge. Such knowledge can then be used to design appropriate manuals and training materials for each group of users. These are then sorted into classifications.

Question 6.2

Perform a Task analysis for knowledge description analysis of using the library to borrow books, using both students and library staff. Use card-sorting techniques to obtain the views of the two groups. In what respects do the views differ?

6.2 Conceptual modelling

Techniques such as Soft Systems Methodology (SSM) have emphasised the need for conceptual modelling of systems users. In other words, we need to understand the ways that different system users and potential users understand and make-sense-of the system and its components. Only by finding out about user perceptions and expectations can we predict the kind of actions users will try. Methods such as COMPACT and Multiview have incorporated SSM into their systems development methods in an attempt to identify some of these issues. Designers can use DFDs to represent users' conceptual knowledge of procedures, and E-R diagrams to represent the structure of their knowledge. DFDs can fairly easily be explained to end users, who can then check that they adequately represent the system from their viewpoint. Once DFDs have been checked with end-users tasks can be analysed for their suitability for computer or human processing, and DFDs can be amended to show the allocation of tasks to either people or computers. Hierarchical Task Analysis using Jackson Structured Diagrams can represent the sub-components of tasks, and can form the basis for the design of manuals and training courses. HTA can also be used to analyse old and new tasks to identify areas where training is required. Task Analysis for Knowledge Description can be used to investigate user views of task structures, and to identify appropriate training materials for different user groups.

However, when we look at techniques for representing user and context characteristics, there is much less available in the way of toolsets and notations. Instead, we are offered various checklists of characteristics such as the National Physical Laboratory's Context of Use Questionnaire which considers factors such as computing experience, level of qualifications, age, gender, motivation to use product, noise, temperature and humidity levels etc. It is generally much harder to find ways of adequately representing such contextual knowledge of tasks.

6.3 User needs analysis: what are we trying to design, and for whom?

An early approach to task design was that associated with F W Taylor at the beginning of the twentieth century. He believed that the laws of science could be applied to job design, and that the task of managers was to design-out all the decision-making,, leaving workers with clear sets of instructions in minute detail as to how they were to perform their tasks. Taylor assumed that the sole motivator for workers was money (rather like some performance related pay schemes today, perhaps?). These approaches, known as Scientific Management, were applied in early twentieth century manufacturing, notably in car manufacturing, with dramatic increases in productivity. However, since the 1920s Taylor's ideas have been challenged, notably by the Hawthorne studies in the USA in the 1920s, which found that factors other than money motivated workers, and that human work behaviour was much more complex than Taylor supposed. The socio-technical approach represents an attempt to apply this alternative view of work and motivation in the design of computer systems, as we saw when ETHICS was discussed above.

In Chapter 2 we introduced some of the issues when considering tasks that systems should perform and the need to take account of different types of user. We saw that many cognitive approaches assumed rational human users who always adopted the most efficient strategies to achieve task goals, but we also saw that these assumptions were very wide of the mark as far as real users are concerned. We have also seen that often the requirements gathering stage of development involves the marketing department of a software design organisation talking to the senior managers of the client company, rather than human factors-aware systems designers talking to real end-users of the system. The approaches to systems development which take account of social and organisational factors, such as ETHICS and Multiview have shown that there is often competition for scarce resources and internal power struggles between different groups in an organisation, quite apart from any real or perceived industrial relations implications that new systems might have. As more work environments embrace computer-supported co-operative working (CSCW) these issues become even more important. Approaches to systems design which ignore these issues are unlikely to produce usable systems.

6 Designing interfaces

Answer 6.1   *Task analysis observes and records actual behaviour, whereas GOMS constructs a model of behaviour based on fairly unrealistic assumptions about users. See Chapter 7 for more on GOMS.*

Designing Groupware systems for computer-supported co-operative work (CSCW)

Groupware systems produce particular problems, yet expectations are often very high as on the face of it email, for example, seems a much more efficient method of communication than traditional methods. A fundamental reason for the failure of many groupware systems is that those who benefit from the system are not necessarily those who do the work. For example, shared calendars are fine for those managers with secretaries to organise their diaries, but a potential nightmare for subordinates without such secretarial support, especially when many if not most activities of the subordinates are not recorded on the system. In education for example, senior staff will often have a workload made up almost entirely of meetings, recorded in diaries (either paper or electronic). However, junior staff will typically have a workload made up of a combination of teaching, preparing classes, marking work, seeing students and colleagues, research etc., most of which would not normally be recorded in diaries or calendars. Forcing such staff to record on a groupware system all such details significantly increases their workload yet it is the senior manager who wishes to arrange a meeting at short notice who benefits from the system. Attempting to force the use of such systems only increases resistance and is likely to de-motivate junior staff. Whenever groupware systems are being designed, it is essential to ensure that if the user has an increased task load as a result of the system they also obtain some benefits from it.

Another problem with groupware systems is that they may reduce the rate of participation of system contributors since the social pressures to contribute are different from those in a face-to-face meeting where it is easier to keep track of who has and who hasn't made a contribution to the meeting. Alternatively, there is the same lack of social pressure to restrain those who have a tendency to 'contribute' too much and too often. There is also the problem of passing control between users since the usual non-verbal cues such as eye contact, direction of gaze, body movements, uhms and errs etc. are not available, although the emerging video conferencing systems that allow moving video images of several users may go some way towards solving some of these problems.

A further problem with email systems is that until large numbers of people are using it, it is ineffective, yet because it is ineffective, people don't use it, a classic chicken-and-egg type problem. All too often users enthusiastically log-on at the start of each day to their new email system, only to find no messages, so after a few days they don't bother checking their mail, thereby reducing the immediacy (the main benefit) of the system. However, this can be solved by running the mail program as a background task that displays a message box when a mail item arrives.

Groupware systems also affect power relationships in organisations. Many tasks can now be completed as effectively by workers working from home, with the benefit to the company that smaller premises, less furniture etc. is required. Home working also allows those with disabilities that make commuting difficult to hold down a normal job. Advantages to the individual include the time not spent commuting, the cost of fares, petrol etc. On the face of it, there appear to be no losers from home working. However, managers and supervisors of workers who now work from home may feel that their role has been diminished and may be strongly opposed to the introduction of home working for such reasons. If the dominant managerial style is one where objectives are set and workers left to get on with the tasks, there should be no problem. But where the style is one of control and looking over the shoulder, problems can be anticipated.

Home working could also have serious implications for the culture of the workplace, including the absence of opportunities for informal meetings and contacts to occur in the workplace. Those companies who try to foster feelings of belonging to one big family, such as many Japanese companies, may find it much more difficult with widespread home working. There are also serious implications for trade union organisation, not to mention the impact on those who provide services to commuters such as transport organisations, cafes and restaurants etc. We should not forget that the introduction of the factory as the normal place of work instead of the home during the industrial revolution was more to do with being able to control the pace of work (and therefore of output) than with optimising efficiency. Just as the industrial revolution had a dramatic effect on women's' roles in work and the home, so a move towards widespread home working could similarly impact on male and female roles next century.

In summary, groupworking systems are not necessary the obvious route to more efficient working that they are sometimes portrayed as. The design of systems for individual tasks is difficult enough, and poorly implemented in the majority of systems. Group work systems introduce a whole new range of additional problems that are only just beginning to be understood let alone solved by systems designers. Before considering such systems, important questions concerning management styles, costs and benefits to all users, and effects on power relationships have to be investigated. Whilst emerging video conferencing systems offer solutions to some of these problems, they are essentially social rather than technological issues.

Question 6.3	What particular factors need to be taken into account when designing groupware systems?

6.4 Organisational factors influencing Interface Design

Information Systems designers (ISDs) and HCI designers come from distinct backgrounds, with different priorities and values.

Software development projects are usually in-house or contracted ISD projects (e.g. UK government projects using SSADM).

Usability concerns, however, stem from the development of commercial software products such as Microsoft Windows or the Apple Macintosh. Since the late 1970s computer users have shifted from a small group of trained users in mini and mainframe environments to widespread untrained users of home and standalone business personal computers. Much of the software for such PCs had more functionality than its typical user could ever make use of, so software houses started to differentiate and market their products in terms of their ease of use rather than functionality. The success of the Apple Macintosh throughout the 1980s, when it regularly took approximately 7% of the personal computer market, has only served to reinforce this strategy.

Software development in such organisations typically occurred in two stages: firstly a marketing-lead phase concerned with product functionality. Only after this phase are the HCI experts brought in to bolt-on an interface to the already specified

Answer 6.3 *Organisational factors are especially important: how will the new system affect power relationships and management styles, do all users benefit, do all users contribute to the system? These questions are often better answered by someone with sociological rather than systems analysis skills*

product. Because of their late involvement, the HCI experts aren't involved in the requirements analysis stage, instead having to design suitable interfaces for unspecified generic users.

In contrast, the in-house development process has as its aim the production of useful systems to perform certain required functions. For reasons rooted in the traditional approach to systems analysis and design (the waterfall model), concern with the interface has usually been relegated to the later stages of development (e.g. stage 5 out of 6 in SSADM). Such an approach to systems design arose in a context (the 1970s) of large-scale computing, with most users being engineers or operators who knew the system or were prepared to learn it. Batch processing was the norm, with very little interactive processing, and the expense of hardware encouraged the view that processor-hungry interfaces should be avoided in favour of adapting the users to the hardware rather than the other way around.

In summary, the assumptions about the development process and the characteristics of system users were quite different for the ISD and HCI approaches to systems development. However, in the late 1980s there emerged a convergence as non-expert end-users started to demand the same levels of usability of software at work as they found on home or standalone machines, and this has forced the ISD approach to change to more user-centred, iterative and participative approaches to systems design.

It has been argued that developers know how to design usable systems, but that organisational obstacles prevent the implementation of such systems. Perhaps the principles of interface design are not applied because developers underestimate the differing needs of different types of users, base decisions on common-sense theories of users rather than on evidence of user behaviour, and believe that end-users don't know what they want anyway. The end result of the current practices of much systems development is the separation of system developers from the end-users, for various reasons concerned largely with organisational practices and values. But as we saw when we looked at systems design methods, and will also see when we consider interface design guidelines and principles, the need for involvement of end-users with the design team at all stages of design is paramount.

6.5 Use of guidelines and style guides

Many guidelines exist, from the general to the very specific. At one extreme, Microsoft's Windows Interface Application Design Guide (Microsoft 1992) states 'An application should be visually, conceptually and linguistically clear'. At the other, Smith & Mosier's guidelines contain 944 detailed and commented guidelines.

Style guides are product-specific guidelines, such as the Open Look, Motif and Apple guidelines, concerned with the application of general principles within the particular environment.

Guidelines are cheap, can be applied early in the design life-cycle, and don't require end-user testing. However, they have a number of disadvantages:

1.   General guidelines are difficult to interpret. Detailed ones tend to be too specific.

2. They often give contradictory advice, and need to be interpreted in context.

3. Guidelines don't necessarily deal with all aspects of a particular interface.

4. They often anticipate theoretical problems which in practice are not experienced by very many end users.

5. Compliance with guidelines doesn't ensure any given level of usability, and is no substitute for usability testing.

Many guidelines pre-date the widespread availability of graphical interfaces such as the Macintosh and Windows interfaces. Chapter eight considers guidelines in more detail.

Overview

This Guide

This Visual Design Guide is a living document intended to describe Microsoft standards for the graphic design of user interface elements. It is primarily intended as a specification of Windows design.

The Guide is divided into five sections: Overview, Windows 3.x System Visuals, Application Visuals, Icon Design, and Resolutions.

Overview
The Overview provides you background design theory and visual perception. The Overview also describes how these principles apply to Windows, standards for screen design, and the use of color and fonts.

Windows 3.x System Visuals
The Windows 3.x System Visuals section describes screen elements provided by the system (Windows). These elements (including buttons, title bars, window frames, and minimize/maximize buttons) combine to create the look and feel of the Windows interface and are a baseline for the design of application screen elements.

Application Visuals
The Application Visuals section includes some graphic elements of an interface not pre-defined by the system, including graphic buttons, toolbars, toolboxes and cursors.

Application Examples
The Applications Examples section presents the most current application interfaces within the Windows 3.x standards.

The opening screen of the Microsoft Visual Basic on-line style guide

6.5.1 Interface Design Principles: Gould and Lewis

Gould and Lewis have identified the following as the main principles for good interface design:

- Early focus on users. Developers need direct contact with end users in order to understand users' mental maps of their tasks and work environment

- Early, iterative user testing. Nothing can prepare us for actual user behaviour, so there is no substitute for actual testing with typical end-users.

- Iterative design. Prototype design, user testing, feedback and re-design continually until acceptance criteria are met.

- Integrated design. All aspects of usability should take place in parallel. The design of the interface, training materials, manuals, on-line help etc. should all be integrated.

6.5.2 Heuristics

Heuristics differ from guidelines in that they are much more general (and shorter!) and are intended to guide designers to look out for the kinds of errors that will reduce the usability of interfaces. The best-known heuristics are those produced and tested by Molich and Nielsen, shown below.

Molich & Nielsen's Heuristics for dialogue design

> "Human-computer dialogue construction appears deceptively simple, yet it is full of subtle pitfalls". R. Molich & J. Nielsen.

The above quote, used at the start of this book, sums up the heart of the problem of interface design. Much of what has been written about interface design seems so obvious that we are often tempted to say 'so what?', yet investigations of software designers show that much of our knowledge of good interface design is poorly understood and implemented by software designers. Molich and Nielsen's heuristics have been developed and tested since the late 1980s and have been shown to be able both to identify potential interface problems and to evaluate quickly and cheaply completed human-computer interfaces.

1. **Use simple and natural dialogue**

   Dialogues should not contain irrelevant or rarely needed information. Extraneous information competes with the relevant pieces of information and diminishes their relative visibility. All information should appear in a natural and logical order. For example, information about the version number of software, or the user ID number isn't usually relevant beyond start-up screens, so shouldn't be repeated in other screens.

2. **Speak the user's language**

   The dialogue should be expressed clearly in words, phrases and concepts familiar to the user rather than in system-oriented terms. For example, messages such as 'illegal entry' or 'Segment load failure' will not make sense to most end-users of systems.

3. **Minimise the user's memory load**

   Short-term memory is limited. The user should not have to remember information from one part of the dialogue to another. Instructions for use of the system should be visible or easily retrievable whenever appropriate. Complicated instructions should be simplified.

4. **Be consistent**

   Users should not have to wonder whether different words, situations or actions mean the same thing. Sub-systems should similarly be co-ordinated and consistent. For example, if you are using 'Exit' to leave the program, then don't use 'Quit' in other parts of the application.

5. Provide feedback

The system should keep the user informed about what is going on by providing him or her with appropriate feedback within a reasonable time. After about 15 seconds, users start to get anxious if nothing appears to have happened, and will probably start repeating their actions (a typical problem with network printers, a user sends a file to the printer, nothing appears to happen so they send it again). The use of moving bar charts or dials to show the percentage of the action that has been completed is a way of providing such feedback, for example in the installation routines of much Windows software.

6. **Provide clearly marked exits**

    Users often choose system options by mistake, and will need a clearly marked escape path to leave the unwanted state. There should always be an 'Exit' option clearly available (for example, on a File menu).

7. **Provide shortcuts**

    Features that make a system easy to learn are often cumbersome for experienced users. Clever shortcuts, unseen by the novice user, may often be included in a system so that it caters for both novice and experienced users. For example, the use of the CTRL-END keys to move to the end of a long Word for Windows file rather than the scroll bars or Page Down key.

8. **Provide good error messages**

    Good error messages are defensive, blaming the problem on the system rather than the user; they should provide precise information about the cause of the error, and meaningful suggestions to the user about what to do next. Messages such as 'Illegal Command!' do little or nothing to help end users, and in so far as they are likely to raise anxiety levels, will actually hinder the user in selecting the correct action to perform.

9. **Error prevention**

    Even better than good error messages is careful design that prevents a problem from occurring in the first place. For example, the referential integrity feature of many relational database packages prevents users from accidentally deleting data from one file that is still required in another (although error messages explaining why the action isn't allowed by the system often fall short in terms of heuristic 8 above).

Studies by Molich and Nielsen using their heuristics have shown that on average five evaluators will find about 80% of interface problems, but increasing the number of evaluators above five leads to fewer and fewer new problems being found and is not recommended as cost effective. They also found that serious interface problems only required two or three evaluators. However, if there is only one evaluator they are unlikely to find more than around 30% of problems. The evaluators need not be HCI experts, either. They can instead be computer scientists or software designers with a small amount of training. They recommend that four or five evaluators are used. Their conclusion is that it is more effective to have more iterations using a small number of evaluators to asses each prototype than to have fewer iterations with a greater number of evaluators. Chapter 8 discusses the use of heuristics for the evaluation (as opposed to the design) of interfaces.

```
┌─────────────────────────────────────────────────────────────┐
│                                                               │
│    REQ094         HILL.BOOKREQ RELEASE 3.3      USER=JANECROC  │
│                                                               │
│                                                               │
│             ***********************************************   │
│                    LIBRARY BOOK REQUEST SYSTEM                │
│             ***********************************************   │
│                                                               │
│    AUTHER                        TITLE                        │
│    >  HILL                       >                            │
│    >  SP                         >                            │
│                                  >                            │
│     STATUS                                                    │
│                                                               │
│          ENTER REQUIRED BOOK DETAILS AND RETURN               │
│                                                               │
│                                                               │
│                                                               │
│    F10=HELP  F7=AUTHORS                    F3=OTHER SERVICES   │
│    F8=TITLES F5=SITES                                         │
└─────────────────────────────────────────────────────────────┘
```

Question 6.4

The above interface is for a book request system for a library. This is the user start-up screen, on which end-users of the library enter details of the book they require. On entering the details, there is a delay of 30 seconds while the system searches for the book requested, before showing its status. If the book isn't in the library catalogue the message 'ILLEGAL ENTRY' appears in the middle of the screen.

You are required to use Molich and Nielsen's list of nine heuristics to see how many faults you can detect with this interface. Write down each fault and identify which of the heuristics it violates.

6.6 Tools for interface development

Many facilities are available to interface designers to aid in the design process, ranging from libraries of procedures for handling specific details of screen displays to user interface management systems (UIMS) featuring a fully-integrated visual development environment and programming language together with library routines, help compilers etc.

Typically, the system interface accounts for around 50% of actual code, and 40-60% of application development time, so anything which raises the productivity of interface coding will have a big impact on overall development time.

UIMSs not only improve productivity, but they also help to ensure consistency of the interface through the provision of standard screen objects such as buttons, controls, dialogue boxes etc. They can also help to avoid copyright problems since the UIMS licence usually makes clear what objects can be freely copied and distributed to users.

6.6.1 Object-oriented programming and interface development.

Object-oriented programming (OOP) languages contain features such as *inheritance*, *encapsulation* and *polymorphism* (see next page for definitions of these terms) which make them particularly suitable for interface development. They allow easy construction of screen objects by the re-use of existing code, they are less likely to suffer from bugs, and the user (and programmer) doesn't have to concern themselves with the fine detail of how the code actually works. They also present visual, direct-manipulation, WYSIWYG development environments that better allow the developer to concentrate on the design aspects of the interface. Examples of OOP languages include C++ and Smalltalk. Languages such as Visual Basic exhibit some of the properties of OOP languages, but are event-driven rather than true OOP languages.

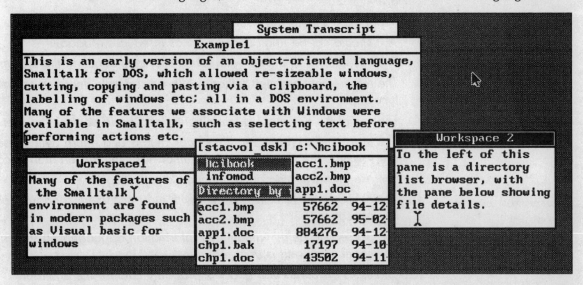

Sample Smalltalk display from a mid-1980s version, showing many of the features associated with the Windows and Macintosh environments, but in a DOS environment.

Inheritance allows a general piece of code to be written for a screen object such as a menu or a dialogue box. For example, code could be written for a Windows File menu. The File menu is an instance of the class of objects menus. An Edit menu can then be written simply by defining the Edit menu as an instance of the Menu class of objects, in which case it inherits all the properties of the Menu class. The code for a menu only needs to be written the once. If at a later stage the developer decided to change some characteristic of the menus, such as changing the default colours, this could be done for all menus just by changing the properties of the menu class definition.

Inheritance allows the re-use of tried-and-tested code as far as possible, thereby avoiding the problems of bugs and unexpected side-effects associated with new code. New features can be added to objects by declaring them as sub-classes of the main class, and adding any necessary features to the sub-class. New instances of sub-classes can of course, be declared, and these will inherit all the characteristics of the parent sub-class. We can think of the use of templates in a wordprocessor as an example of inheritance; by selecting a particular template, our new document is inheriting all the information about margins, headers, footers, fonts for normal and heading text etc.

Encapsulation describes the way in which all the attributes, variables and functions that describe a real-world or screen object are attached to (encapsulated in) that object. The actual workings of the object are hidden from the programmer and from other objects, thereby removing a common cause of bugs due to un-anticipated side effects of code (such as where, in a procedural language, a piece of code might inadvertently change a particular variable). In Visual basic for Windows we use encapsulation each time we create a new screen object such as a text box or command button.

Answer 6.4

The following isn't necessarily an exhaustive list.

1. *The use of release information adds unnecessary clutter the screen and serves no purpose for the user*
2. *The name of the user is unnecessary, as the user probably knows who they are!*
3. *Information should not be truncated where there is sufficient space.*
4. *Text should not be in all upper case as it reduces readability.*
5. *The mis-spelling of author will reduce user confidence in the system.*
6. *The requirement to enter author details on separate lines serves no useful function.*
7. *The use of the > symbol is meaningless and could confuse the user.*
8. *The instruction to 'Enter required book details and return' will cause some users to type the word return; the author has seen this on many occasions.*
9. *The use and grouping of the function keys is illogical.*
10. *Using F10 for Help is inconsistent with most accepted standards for function key allocation.*
11. *The 30 second delay without any information appearing on screen will cause anxiety in users and is unacceptable.*
12. *'Status' is system jargon and will probably confuse the end-user.*
13. *The error message 'ILLEGAL ENTRY' is not user-friendly and provides no information as to why the entry is not accepted.*
14. *There is no indication of how the user exits from the system on the screen.*
15. *There is no facility to cancel a request. This is important given that it takes 30 seconds to process requests, and users will make errors.*
16. *The screen provides no information as to what users should do when they have obtained the information requested.*

Polymorphism refers to the ability to define general procedures such as 'Print' without the need to define specific parameters. For example, obtaining a printout of a bit mapped graphical object is a very different action from obtaining a printout of a small text file, but polymorphism allows the same 'Print' instruction to be used in both cases. Encapsulation ensures that the complexities of the different parameters necessary for actually obtaining the printout are hidden from the user.

The concept of polymorphism is already familiar to users of modern Windows applications even if the term itself is unfamiliar; for example clicking the print icon in programs such as Wordperfect, Excel or Word is an example of polymorphism in that it doesn't matter to the user whether they're printing an Excel chart or worksheet or a word-processed document.

OOP languages such as Smalltalk tend to produce relatively inefficient code and to require large run-time overlays compared to procedural languages such as C. C++ is really a hybrid procedural language with OOP extensions, although it can offer the best of both worlds. As hardware increases in power and users become used to operating environments such as Windows with large hardware requirements, the relative disadvantages of true OOP languages such as Smalltalk begin to disappear. Despite the fact that Smalltalk is over 20 years old, it may only be in the second half of the 1990s that its strengths as a development tool are increasingly recognised.

Question 6.5   What are the benefits for interface designers in using an OOP environment?

6.6.2 Event-driven programming

Traditional procedural languages such as Pascal, Basic and C work by performing each instruction in the program sequentially, then moving on to the next instruction (or branching to another specified part of the program) until all instructions in the program have been executed.

Event-driven programs behave quite differently. Their normal status is to wait for an 'event' to occur. they then process the event (which may typically be a user action such as clicking on a control button or menu etc.) and then wait for the next event. Events are messages that the system or user sends to the program objects (menus, windows, boxes, buttons etc.). Each object encapsulates (see the above section on OOP languages) the details of how it is to respond to messages. Event-driven languages are sometimes confused with OOP languages, but event-driven languages such as Visual Basic for Windows generally only offer some of the features of an OOP, for example Visual Basic offers many pre-defined classes of objects for the Windows environment, which encapsulate appropriate attributes, but it doesn't offer the same extensive class inheritance features of Smalltalk. In practice, however, such fine theoretical distinctions are likely to be unimportant for the interface developer.

6.6.3 Communication between applications and code re-use

Environments such as Windows allow data from one application to be dynamically linked or embedded in another, to the point where eventually a user won't need to actually think about which application they are currently using since clicking on the text or graphical object that they want to manipulate will automatically start-up the associated application. Such a document-centred (rather than application centred) approach will fit in better with the conceptual models of end-users. In programming and interface development terms, it will mean the developer making available a common set of screen objects such as menu bars, control buttons etc. across a range of 'documents' using the encapsulation facilities of environments such as Visual Basic. The use of common shared objects and code re-use that this allows not only reduces development time but also ensures consistency across applications and reduces the likelihood of software bugs and the need for associated software maintenance.

6.6.4 Motif and X-Windows

X-windows allows relatively low-powered graphics terminals to run programs remotely on much more powerful centralised client machines. It was developed as a graphical environment for distributed UNIX systems. Motif provides a library of graphical objects, known as Widgets, which are arranged in an object-oriented hierarchy of classes. Motif programs are event-driven, with the system looking up a database of properties to see what action to take on an object in response to an event. Writing a Motif program is a hybrid of standard procedural text-based coding in C but with calls to event loops which control the behaviour of the widgets.

Motif provides some of the features of OOP and event-driven approaches, but in an only partially visual environment, and with a requirement to write substantial parts of the program in procedural code.

Features such as inheritance, encapsulation and polymorphism allow more rapid development, and encourage modularity and code re-use, both of which are desirable software engineering practices.

6.6.5 HyperCard and the Apple Macintosh

HyperCard is an object-oriented visual programming language for the creation of virtual on-screen 'cards' that can be controlled with buttons and which can contain text fields, graphics and sound. It is aimed at the user who wants to create simple applications such as a flat-file database name and address book. HyperCard programs are called stacks because they use the idea of a stack of index cards, which are created by selecting from menus, typing in text into text fields, and dragging buttons to the appropriate positions. HyperCard can also be used for simple hypertext systems, using buttons to link to another card in the stack.

HyperCard offers a very simple intuitive environment for developing simple applications that fit in with the stack of cards metaphor such as any information that can be stored in a free-form database format. However it is not suitable for developing complete general applications since it only produces programs that look like Hyper-Card stacks and does not give access to the standard Macintosh screen objects. It can be used for developing a rapid prototype interface, but it generally makes more sense to develop such prototypes in an environment that allows their refinement and use in the final program rather than having to throw away the prototype and start interface development proper from scratch in a different environment.

6.6.6 Visual Basic for windows

Visual Basic builds on many of the ideas of Hypercard, but extends them to a fully-fledged development environment.

Visual Basic combines an event-driven language with a visual direct-manipulation development environment. Interface development involves dragging controls for boxes, buttons, menus and all the other common Windows screen objects and placing them on the development screen. The characteristics such as box and button names are entered into properties boxes, with short pieces of code being written to control the behaviour of the object. Third-party developers have already created large numbers of additional controls which can be incorporated in applications. The Professional edition of the program even includes an installer routine using a Microsoft 'wizard' to create an installation disk or disks for the user which they can install just by running SETUP.EXE from the floppy disk. There is also a help compiler to allow developers to write text files that can be turned into a standard windows help system, and a visual design guide with hints and tips on designing windows interfaces.

Visual basic is interpreted rather than complied, so programs written in it run more slowly than those written in C. Nevertheless, it is possible to write programs in Visual Basic and to re-write speed critical routines in C. Another approach is to use Visual Basic to develop the interface but to write the program in C, which allows the use of the same interface objects in prototype and final versions of the system.

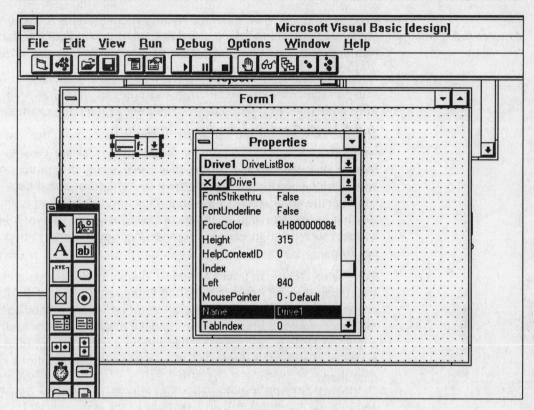

The Visual Basic environment: a drive box has been dragged onto the form and its properties are about to be set in the properties box.

6.7 Supporting design

Support for the design process involves a range of factors which enable software developers to consistently produce better quality interfaces. It includes the following:

Guidance: Guidelines, style guides etc. The use of house or other appropriate style guides, such as those produced by IBM, Motif, Apple or Microsoft. If none of these are appropriate, there are more general guidelines such as those produced by Smith and Mosier and Ravden and Johnston. Molich and Nielsen's heuristics are probably the most usable general guidelines.

Acceptance criteria. An important part of any software development process is knowing when to stop further iterations of the development life-cycle. The establishment of measurable criteria for acceptance gives developers clear goals.

Measures of usability; Health and Safety and ISO standards. Availability of definitive requirements such as the emerging ISO 9241 or EEC 90/270 provide clear statements of at least some of the interface criteria.

Support for communication. As most development occurs within teams, it is important to provide meeting rooms, recording devices for recording interaction with users and the design team etc. Video-conferencing systems allow geographically remote team members to interact face-to-face and brainstorm using facilities such as shared 'whiteboards' displayed on each participants PC.

Software support: capturing ideas and turning them into programs or prototypes, for example with the use of program generators that can turn diagrammatic notations into executable code. User Interface Management Systems (UIMSs) such as Visual Basic, Hypercard and Garnet (for X-windows) provide powerful interface development environments incorporating some of the features of object-orientation.

Access to examples of other systems. Evidence suggests that designers can understand usability factors better from examples of interfaces with good usability than from guidelines etc., so access to databases of interface examples could be useful.

The use of standardised notations helps team communication and communication with other designers. Data flow diagrams (DFDs) are easy to draw and represent inputs, outputs, processes and datastores using the same notation regardless of whether the tasks are to be performed by humans or computers. They are particularly useful at the requirements gathering stage and can be used to represent the system to existing users. We can then decompose activities down into lower-level DFDs, adding more detail at each successive level until we don't need any further decomposition.

Completed DFDs can then be used to identify individual data elements in the system which can then be represented using Entity-relationship (E-R) diagrams to show how system entities ('things' that we are interested in) are related to one another. The E-R diagrams provide a logical system model that can then very easily be implemented as a relational database system, which will be a suitable form of implementation for the majority of typical systems. We can also record descriptions of the data in a data dictionary.

The use of DFDs, E-R diagrams and data dictionaries enable designers to represent what is required, without them having to tie themselves to a particular method of implementation, and without requiring the allocation of tasks to computers and humans prematurely.

Review questions

1. How does task analysis differ from cognitive modelling approaches?

2. How can user needs be incorporated in systems design?

3. How useful are guidelines, heuristics and style guides in the design of the interface?

4. Why are object-oriented development tools particularly useful in interface design?

Test questions

1. What tools and techniques should a systems designer use for the development of user-friendly systems for small and medium systems?

7 Psychological models of usability

7.1 Introduction

In this chapter we shall be reviewing definitions of usability and its relationship to user needs before going on to look in detail at the following approaches to the evaluation of system usability:

- analytic evaluation of design specifications, derived from psychological models of human information processing

- controlled laboratory experiments of specific aspects of system use, to test hypotheses about the design

7.2 Definitions of usability

Before we can try to measure usability we need to know what it is. Most definitions of usability take as their starting point Shackel's (1986) definition as the Learnability, Effectiveness, Flexibility and Attitude. Shackel has tried to come up with a practical definition of usability, measured by setting performance targets at the system design stage for the following criteria:

Effectiveness

- at better than some pre-set level of performance (e.g. in terms of speed and errors),

- by some pre-set percentage of the specified target range of users,

- within some pre-set proportion of the range of usage environments.

Learnability

- within some specified time from installation and start of user training,

- based upon some specified amount of training and user support,

Flexibility

- with flexibility allowing adaptation to some specified percentage variation in tasks and/or environments beyond those first specified.

Attitude

- within acceptable levels of human cost in terms of tiredness, discomfort, frustration and personal effort.

The International Standards Organisation propose that:

> "The usability of a product is the degree to which specific users can achieve specific goals within a particular environment; effectively, efficiently, comfortably, and in an acceptable manner." (Booth 1989 p110).

Eason suggests that the major indicator of usability is whether a system or a feature is in fact used, and that usability can only be tested in the field rather than analytically or in a laboratory. The major disadvantage with such an approach is that in order to assess usability we would have to build the system and then measure to what extent it (and its features) were in fact used in real settings. Clearly such a view of usability is of no help to system designers at the design stage.

7.3 Problems with current definitions of usability:

Most definitions of usability concern themselves with 'products' rather than with systems, and still treat software in isolation from its context of use to a greater or lesser degree, albeit acknowledging the importance of contextual factors.

Question 7.1   What is wrong with Eason's approach to usability?

7.4 Acceptance of definitions of usability

One way to deal with the issue of competing definitions of usability is to investigate the extent to which a particular definition is accepted by the HCI experts. Such a study has been undertaken for the draft ISO 9241 part 10-Dialogue Principles standard. Of those who replied to the survey:

- 81% felt the standard promoted a user-centred approach

- 64% felt it provided a framework for the design and evaluation of dialogue systems

- 74% agreed with the theoretical foundations of the standard

- 58% felt it was mature enough to be published as an international recommendation

- 66% felt it would promote developments in dialogue systems design.

Another survey of current usability engineering practice in Europe found that software designers saw usability in terms of quick, easy training, intuitiveness and ease of use, but that the concept of usability hasn't been defined adequately for those involved in the design of systems. Such designers showed awareness of the need for usability testing, but this was often conducted in informal and superficial ways. The survey concluded that much usability practice is superficial and that the development of standards would be of benefit to designers.

Question 7.2   How far are HCI experts agreed on what usability is, and how far do system developers ensure usability in their systems?

It is proposed that a working definition of usability adds two more dimensions to those of the ISO:

- Conformance to existing and proposed Health and Safety directives and legislation such as, in Europe, the EEC 90/270 directive on Display Screen Equipment requirements

- Conformance to relevant copyright and patent legislation in so far as no software should breach such legislation in attempting to deliver usability.

The usability of a product is the degree to which in a particular environment and situation specific users can achieve specific goals effectively, efficiently, comfortably, and in an acceptable manner in the light of any relevant health and safety and patent or copyright legislation applicable in that situation.

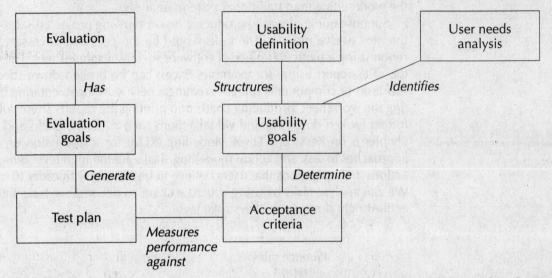

The relationship between usability and evaluation

7.5 User Needs Analysis

The diagram above shows that we need to carry out an analysis of user needs before we can set usability goals and acceptance criteria, so it is appropriate briefly to reconsider user needs analysis before moving on to discuss approaches to evaluation. In Chapter 6 we looked at user needs analysis under the following four headings:

7.5.1 User attributes e.g. novice, expert, occasional etc.

7.5.2 User goals and activities using, for example, Task Analysis

7.5.3 User situation\environment e.g. the work setting

7.5.4 User requirements and preferences e.g. do users prefer keystrokes to mice?

Note that it is important to collect information about users own needs, preferences etc. rather than their manager's (or someone else's) views of their needs.

7.6 End-user tasks and task analysis

Task analysis is concerned with describing what people do in order to achieve their goals, usually in a work context. Task Analysis differs from earlier approaches to systems analysis in that it focuses on end-user's views of what they are trying to achieve and how best to reach their goals rather than formal descriptions based on the view of the systems analyst.

Answer 7.1

Eason's approach can't be used to help in the design of systems, only in their evaluation once completed.

Answer 7.2

Between approximately two thirds and three-quarters of those surveyed agreed with the draft ISO 9241 definition of usability. Developers usually use informal methods to ensure usability

Task Analysis therefore focuses more on the end-user's perceptions and motivations in the work setting than traditional systems analysis.

Suppose our goal was to produce a report showing projected sales of a product for the next twelve months. The tasks would be the activities necessary to produce the report using a particular piece of software such as a spreadsheet. The task (producing the sales report using, for example, Excel) can be broken down (decomposed) into sub-tasks or components such as creating a new worksheet, entering the data, formatting the worksheet, producing charts and printing the report. These sub-tasks are then further broken-down into individual actions such as mouse clicks and key presses-see chapter 6 on Keystroke Level Modelling (KLM) for a discussion of some low level approaches to task and action modelling. Tasks are the high level bundle of motivated actions and operations that users believe to be necessary in order to meet their goals. We can analyse tasks by using structure charts to decompose tasks into sub-tasks and actions right down to the keystroke level.

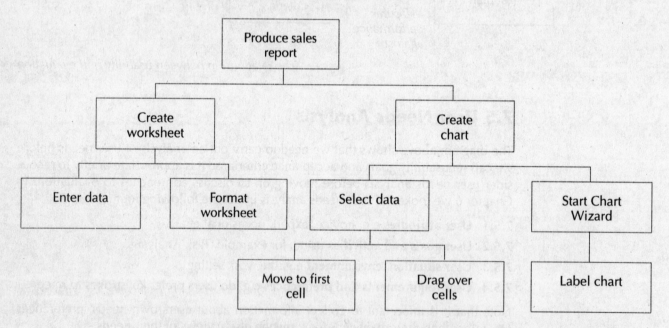

Example of task decomposition chart for producing a projected sales report using Excel. High-level tasks at the top are broken-down into their component tasks.

7.6.1 Representing users' knowledge of tasks

As well as the structure chart notation described above, based on JSP, other diagramming techniques such as Entity-relationship modelling and Data-flow diagrams (DFDs) can be used to model the structure of user's conceptual knowledge of task procedures. DFDs can be used to show tasks and associated flows of data. In conventional systems analysis, DFDs are used to show functional processes that are performed on data. In interface design methods they van be used to take the results of a task decomposition and to show tasks with associated data. Since DFDs use the same symbols for computer and human tasks, they can be used to model tasks before allocating them to either human or computer.

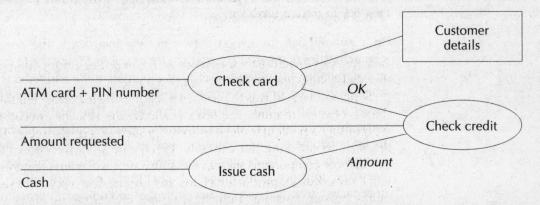

DFD for successful cash machine withdrawal

Entity-relationship diagrams can be used to model the perceived conceptual knowledge that users have of the system and the relationships between the perceived entities. Such models can then be discussed with a range of users and then subject to traditional physical design processes such as data normalisation.

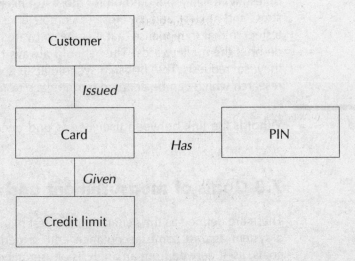

Entity-relationship diagram for a cashcard withdrawal

7.6.2 Conclusions on Task Analysis techniques

The main problem with these approaches is that they are difficult to apply for designers and need to be integrated into a complete analysis and design method (for example, perhaps an extended version of a technique such as Multiview, which is discussed in chapter five, with appropriate interface design extensions). However, we will need to await future developments in this area. For the moment, knowledge of the issues and techniques provides useful background awareness for interface designers, but doesn't provide an integrated set of design techniques.

Since the 1980s the focus of analysis has gradually moved away from detailed psychological models of behaviour, such as GOMS, to concerns with motivational and contextual issues using methods such as cognitive walkthroughs, claims analysis and analysis of stakeholders. There is as yet little evidence that task analysis techniques have been of practical benefit in the design of actual systems.

7.6.3 Cognitive walkthroughs

In a walkthrough the expert determines the exact task, the context, and important characteristics of the user population, for example: 'You want to use the library photocopier number 4 to make one copy of a journal article and reduce the size so that two pages will fit on one sheet of A4 paper. The user is a second-year student but has never used this particular photocopier before'. The evaluator then mentally 'walks through' the actions necessary, attempting to predict user behaviour, problems likely to be encountered and strategies used to solve the problem. Results are recorded using a checklist. Tasks are broken down into goals and sub-goals, and the actions necessary to proceed from one sub-goal to the next, rather like in the more formal approaches to task analysis, but with the addition of information about users and context.

7.7 Ethical issues in testing

One final area to consider before addressing evaluation is the Question of the ethics of testing. It is not uncommon for those testing software to demonstrate high levels of stress and anxiety and to refuse to complete testing! It is important to carefully brief testers so that they realise that it is the software, not them, that is being tested, and to de-brief them afterwards. They should always be allowed to abandon the testing if they so request. The British Psychological Society publish ethical guidelines for research which can be adapted for interface testing.

Question 7.3   What is the link between user needs and acceptance criteria?

7.8 Goals of measurement and evaluation

These are defined as the generation of a test plan which measures the performance of a system against some acceptance criteria derived from a set of situated usability goals, itself derived from an analysis of user needs.

7.9 Methods of evaluation

Whilst there are many individual evaluation techniques, they can be grouped for convenience under the following categories.

Analytic: largely based on psychological models of user tasks.

Expert: Experienced systems analysts and designers evaluate the design before it is shown to end users.

Observational: these can be field or usability-lab based studies of actual users of the system. They typically involve the following:

- Audio and video recording
- Verbal protocols
- Data logging

Survey: Attitude Surveys, rating scales etc. are carried out with users.

Experimental: Laboratory studies to investigate different design elements.

Analytic and expert techniques don't involve evaluation of real end-users. Survey and observational approaches usually occur in natural or near-natural settings, with real users in a typical environment. Experimental approaches use laboratory-like settings with strictly controlled variables in order to investigate the effects of particular aspects of interface design.

Question 7.4

What are the advantages of evaluation methods that don't require prototypes or working systems?

7.10 Analytic evaluation methods

These techniques stem from psychological models of human information processing which view human processes as similar to the processes occurring inside a computer. Two main approaches are those based on psychological models of user behaviour towards goals, exemplified by GOMS (goals, operators, methods and selection rules), and those based on linguistic models that attempt to evaluate the complexity of tasks by constructing a task grammar which can then be used to evaluate task complexity, with less complex tasks being simpler to perform and learn, in the same way that it's easier to understand grammatically simple statements in a foreign language. TAG(task-action grammar) exemplifies this second approach.

Analytic approaches don't require any end-user testing, and they don't even require prototypes but instead are based on analyses of interface specifications. Thus they are very cheap to use and evaluation can take place very early in the life-cycle.

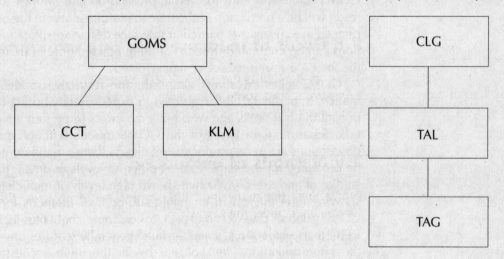

Analytic models in HCI evaluation

Answer to 7.3	*An analysis of user needs is carried out in order to establish usability goals such as '80% of novice users should be able to perform the file open operation within 60 seconds'. These then define the acceptance criteria to be met in usability tests.*
Answer to 7.4	*They can be used earlier in the software life-cycle and are very cheap.*

7.11 GOMS

GOMS stands for goals, operators, methods and selection rules. Tasks are broken-down into their components to predict performance times. GOMS assumes humans act rationally to achieve their goals, that users know which actions to perform, and that performance is error-free with no allowance for any problem-solving behaviour. In other words, that all users are experts who never make mistakes!

The user's mental model is assumed to be made up of goals, operators, methods and a set of selection rules for choosing between different methods.

- **Goals** are objectives e.g. to locate a spelling mistake.

- **Methods** are descriptions of procedures for achieving goals stored in the user's long-term memory and are part of his/her knowledge structure of the task built-up from past experience and learning (hence the assumption of error-free performance with no allowances for problem-solving). For example, knowledge of ways to locate spelling mistakes in a particular word processor.

- **Operators** are actions that change the system state or the user's cognitive state, for example USE MENU TO LOCATE SPELL CHECKER

- **Selection rules** are IF...THEN statements to enable the user to choose between methods, for example, IF remember shortcut key THEN use it, ELSE use menu.

To use GOMS to evaluate a design the analyst has to perform a task analysis using the GOMS framework and to then apply appropriate timings to each action. The end result will be a prediction of the time to perform a task in the optimal way, by an experienced user, using that particular interface design specification. Alternative specifications can be compared in terms of the predicted time to perform identical tasks, and the 'best' (fastest) interface design selected.

GOMS relies on a very simplistic and restrictive model of human task performance. In particular, it is restricted to expert users who act rationally at all times in pursuit of clear goals and who make no errors in performance. It relies on full, clear task descriptions in terms of the GOMS model, without specifying how such task descriptions are to be produced, yet clearly there are different descriptions that could be produced for the same goal, at differing levels of detail. In contrast observational studies of end users have often shown high levels of inefficient behaviour, with users showing little interest in changing sub-optimal methods for optimal ones. From a GOMS analysis one would expect, for example, that Lotus 123 version 2 would score lower than Supercalc 4, since the latter generally requires fewer keystrokes to perform the same operations. Yet Lotus is by far the more successful product, with Lotus scoring more highly on usability than Supercalc in a recent test (PC-UK magazine, 1992).

Question 7.5	How realistic are the GOMS assumptions?

Question 7.6   Why might a software package that required less keystrokes to perform an operation achieve a better rating using GOMS than another package requiring more keystrokes? Why might this give a false view of usability?

7.12 Keystroke Level Model (KLM)

The Keystroke Level Model is derived from GOMS, and describes the time taken to execute sub-tasks using the system's facilities. Total time taken for an action is arrived at by simply adding together the times for each component task. The following table gives typical timings for various operations:

Press key	
Good typist (90 wpm)	0.12 sec
Poor typist (40 wpm)	0.28 sec
Non-typist	1.20 sec
Mouse click	0.20 sec
Point with mouse	1.10 sec
Move hands to keyboard	0.40 sec

Timings for various actions in KLM (adapted from Card, Moran & Newell 1983).

KLM breaks task execution down into the following operations: keystroke (K), pointing (P), homing (H-moving hand1s to key, mouse etc.), drawing (D-no typical timings are given since this varies with task), mental operation (M-the slight pause as the user recalls what to do next), and system response time (R).

KLM is in effect a low-level GOMS model where the method is given. Like GOMS it is unable to take account of task learning, and assumes that all complex tasks are sub-divided into simple sub-tasks. It is assumed that users have already decided what actions to perform, and how to perform them.

Question 7.7   Which is faster for poor typists, pressing ALT-F-O to open a file, or pointing to a file open icon on a toolbar and clicking?

Question 7.8   Which style, keystrokes or mice, is likely to appeal most to a good typist?

KLM is subject to the same limitations as the GOMS model from which it is derived, that it assumes expert users who know what they want to do and how they want to do it. However, it can be used to compare two or more interface specifications to see which one is fastest. But we should not assume that fastest is best, and KLM is of no use with non-expert users. Since increasingly non-expert end-users are expected to use systems on a regular basis, the KLM model would appear to be of limited use.

Answer to 7.5   *GOMS assumes expert users who never make mistakes, yet even experts will make mistakes sometimes. GOMS can't tell us anything about novice or casual users of the system.*

Answer to 7.6   *GOMS is based on adding-up the timings required to perform the keystrokes necessary, so the product with less keystrokes will have a better score. But real users may have problems remembering the keystrokes, whilst a different package may require more keystrokes but they may be easier to remember.*

Answer to 7.7   *3×0.28 secs = 0.84, pointing =1.10 secs, so keystrokes will be faster, But for a non-typist, pointing will be much faster, over 3 times as quick.*

Answer to 7.8   *Most operations will be faster using keystrokes unless they require 7 or more keystrokes for one point-and-click operation.*

Perhaps its main contribution is in the provision of data concerning complex sequences of mouse actions that can show the potential time advantage of providing a keyboard shortcut, for example one could carry out a KLM analysis of the time to move from page one to the end of page 10 of a Word for Windows document using mouse and scroll bar actions; menu actions and the CTRL-END shortcut to show the speed advantage of teaching users the keyboard shortcut. Such an analysis would not require either users or the software, just an interface specification and typical timings for the actions. A software designer faced with an interface specification that required long sequences of direct manipulation actions could carry out a KLM analysis to see the benefit of providing a keyboard shortcut. However, it has been shown that many non-expert users aren't interested in learning shortcuts, preferring to stick with less efficient methods that they feel comfortable with.

Question 7.9   When might a designer use a KLM evaluation?

7.13 Cognitive Complexity Theory (CCT)

Cognitive Complexity Theory is an extension of GOMS. It attempts to predict how difficult to learn and use a system will be based on a GOMS model of the task and its required knowledge, a model of the user's current knowledge, and a list of the items of knowledge to be learned in order for the user to be able to make error-free use of the system. The user's knowledge is modelled using production rules with the general form:

IF <condition>THEN<action>

For example,

IF
        <goal is to drive to London>
THEN
        <do sequence>
        <start car>
        <drive to M>
        <take M6 South direction>

Training time is calculated by the following formula:

training time = t × n + c

where t= training time per production rule
n= number of new production rules to be learned to reach goal
c= time required for already-learned part of the task

Each new production rule is assumed to take the same amount of time to learn. Performance is calculated by simply counting the number of production rules and the task execution times.

CCT suffers from the same limitations as the GOMS model from which it is derived. Additionally, the assumption that all production rules take the same time to learn ignores the different degrees of complexity of rules. Once again, it is assumed that users perform tasks in the optimal way, with no allowances made for errors.

7.14 Conclusions on GOMS, KLM and CCT

These three related methods each try to predict performance based on time taken to perform standard actions and time taken to learn necessary new task knowledge. They can be applied to a specification only and do not require either end users or even a prototype interface. However, the methods are difficult to apply, have not been found to help interface design in practice, and are based on unrealistic assumptions concerning human behaviour, notably that humans always behave rationally, and always choose optimal strategies to perform tasks.

However, these techniques can be used to analyse complex mouse sequences and to compare likely performance for expert users when keyboard shortcuts are provided. As such, they can help designers identify where such keyboard shortcuts may offer the greatest potential productivity gains, but many users are content to stick with their own sub-optimal strategies.

As software tools for interface prototyping such as Visual Basic for Windows become more readily available the advantages of being able to predict performance from specifications rather than from prototypes will become less significant.

Question 7.10

Why might the advantage of being able to predict performance become less important in future?

Language-based evaluation models

7.15 Command Language Grammar (CLG)

Command Language Grammar (Moran 1981) is an attempt to provide designers with a model of the tasks users need to perform which are then broken-down into sub-tasks and descriptions of necessary actions.

CLG has four levels:

• **Task:** concerned with task aims such as 'How can I use the system to update a cash flow forecast'

• **Semantic:** concerned with 'How do I delete the projected figures for March?'

To decide which keyboard shortcuts should be available for commonly performed operations such as moving to the beginning or end of a word processor document.

Because of the greater availability of interface prototyping tools such as Visual Basic for Windows, so that actual working prototypes can be tested with real users.

- **Syntactic:** concerned with what the displays should be like-'How do I select the required cell?'

- **Interaction:** 'Which keys or buttons do I press to delete the old figure?'. Two further projected levels, spatial and device, have not been developed in CLG.

CLG produces a task hierarchy model, with tasks broken down into sub-tasks in a structured way, rather like s structure chart. At the semantic level, pseudocode is used to describe entities and permissible actions. The syntactic level uses commands which contain arguments, which refer to the entities. The interaction level specifies commands that are available in that context or screen. It provides the rule structure and command set for the user interaction.

The different levels are described using pseudocode with conventional programming language control constructs such as IF.....THEN.....ELSE, START, STOP etc. As you can imagine, it is very difficult and time consuming to represent the cash flow forecast example above in CLG.

The intention of CLG is to describe the interface at the design stage, before prototyping. It assumes that some form of task analysis has already been undertaken. The CLG description of the interface is not easy to understand, and no evaluation can be performed on it. Unsurprisingly, Sharratt (1987) in a study of the use of CLG found that designers found it difficult to use, made many errors in specifying the interface using CLG, and that there was no evidence that designs specified using it were superior in any way.

7.16 Task Action Language (TAL)

Task Action Language tries to develop the ideas of CLG by adopting a more formal production rule grammar, Backus-Naur Form (BNF), to allow comparison and evaluation of interface designs at the earliest stages of design. Using BNF it is possible to describe all rules governing interaction in a system in terms of:

1. terminal symbols (the words in the language);

2. non-terminal symbols (invented constructs to show the structure of the language e.g. noun phrase);

3. a starting symbol;

4. meta-symbols for *and, or* and *is composed of*;

5. rules constructed from the above.

Predictions about ease of use can be made based on the assumption that good design involves minimising the number of rules, the lengths of terminal symbols and the number of terminal symbols. Compared with CLG, TAL adopts a more formal notation and uses software metrics. It can be used to describe two designs and to predict which will give the better performance. TAL however lacks a model of the user, and makes the same kinds of assumptions as GOMS regarding rational human actions and error-free performance.

7.17 Task Action Grammar (TAG)

Task Action Grammar (Payne & Green 1986) is a further development of TAL which attempts to evaluate the consistency of the interface, on the assumption that inconsistencies in an interface require additional rules and that the more rules (i.e. rules for 'special cases'), the harder the system is to learn. In effect, evaluation is by counting the number of rules and special cases.

For example, if in a system it was sometimes necessary to specify an action then select the entity on which the action was to be performed, but in other circumstances the entity was first selected and then the action specified, the system would require more rules to describe than one where selection always occurs prior to specifying the action to take, and the former system would be predicted to be more difficult to learn.

A concrete example is the Windows database Superbase 4 version 1.21. In most windows programs, there is an option from the File menu to allow the Renaming of a file, including changing its destination drive. But in Superbase 1.21 no Renaming option is available from the File menu, and the default drive can only be re-assigned from a Set menu. Compared with most other windows products, Superbase needs additional rules to describe the Renaming operations, so a TAG analysis would predict that it would be harder to learn than a product adopting the standard approach.

Like the other analytic models discussed, TAG assumes expert users with perfect knowledge of the so-called 'simple tasks' that can be performed by any user, and for which no allowance is made for task complexity. But there is no method in TAG for selecting which tasks need to be modelled.

Question 7.11

Why, according to TAG, would an inconsistent interface be harder to learn than a consistent one?

7.18 KAT (Knowledge Analysis of Tasks)

KAT involves the following stages:

- Identify the person's goals, sub-goals and sub-tasks.
- Work out order in which sub-goals are to be carried out.
- Identify task strategies.
- Identify Procedures.
- Identify Task Objects and Actions.

KAT emphasises the need to account of the fact that different individuals perform the same tasks, and the need to sample a representative selection of those performing a particular task. Any organisational factors affecting task performance should also be identified, with sampling of tasks across organisations to remove variation due to different organisation types. It is also necessary to identify those aspects of the task which are dependent on particular technologies and those which are independent.

The inconsistent interface requires more rules to describe its operation, and the more rules you need to learn, the harder the I/f is to learn.

Task data are gathered using a variety of techniques including interviews and questionnaires, observation, rating scales, repertory grids and card sorting (to group similar tasks together). The completed task analysis is then checked with task performers. The ultimate aim of KAT is to produce a formal specification for the user interface.

7.19 Conclusions on analytic evaluation models generally

The main strength of such models is that they can be used by designers very early in the life cycle, don't require end users or even prototypes and are therefore cheap to use.

However, they are based on totally unrealistic assumptions, ignore context, are difficult to use, their results are often difficult to interpret, and evaluations of the methods have not revealed any significant advantages to designers using analytic evaluation compared to other methods of evaluation.

Whilst they can be used to compare two or more designs and predict some aspects of learnability and performance without the need for a prototype, their assumptions about users' behaviour combined with the increasing availability of rapid interface prototyping systems and the observed performance of 'Expert' evaluation methods such as heuristics and walkthroughs means that at present they are not an attractive range of practical techniques for interface evaluation.

7.20 Experimental evaluation

Experimental evaluation occurs at the implementation rather than at the specification stage, and is based on psychological experimental techniques.

Such experiments can be used after usability tests with users to try to identify the real nature of observed problems, and to carry out controlled test to investigate particular hypotheses (testable ideas) concerning user problems.

For example, if a usability study revealed that users had problems selecting the correct icon from a toolbar an experiment could be set up with two interfaces identical in all respects except that one toolbar also used text labels beneath the icons (like the labels in Excel 5, for example) whilst the other had no text labels. Matched pairs of users could then perform identical tasks with both interfaces; and performance could be measured to test the hypothesis that those using the labelled toolbar would score higher than those using the un-labelled toolbar. The results could be analysed using statistical tests to see if the observed difference in mean performance score between the two groups was statistically significant.

Designing experiments

Designing HCI experiments involves the following:

1. Formulating the hypotheses.
2. Choosing a means to test the hypotheses.

3. Identifying all variables that might affect the result of the experiment.

4. Determining which are the independent variables (and levels of the independent variable), dependent variables and which variables need to be controlled by some means.

5. Deciding the experimental tasks, design, and data collection method.

6. Subject selection method.

7. Choose appropriate statistical or other analysis technique (see table below).

8. Carrying out a pilot study (i.e. prototype the experimental design).

Typical dependant variables (which should normally be based on metrics of some sort) which are observed and measured in usability experiments include:

- Time taken to complete task
- Number of tasks completed
- Quality of task output
- Number of errors made
- Where (at what point in the task) were the errors made
- Time taken to recover from an error
- Preference ratings and attitude scores
- Waiting time before initiating a response

Experimental Design considerations (adapted from Johnson 1992 p88)

Level within a factor	The particular manipulations within a single dimension (e.g. interface style might have two levels – icons and menus, while level of expertise might have three levels – novice, partial expert, expert).
Between groups design	Different groups of subjects used in each condition of the experiment. (enables asymmetric transfer effects to be controlled.)
Within-groups design	The same group of subjects are used in all conditions of the experiment (where repeated measures on different variables or levels are obtained from each subject).
Mixed-groups design	Some conditions of the experiment are given to the same subjects, but other conditions require different groups of subjects (i.e. a mix of between- and within-group designs).
Longitudinal Study	Same group of subjects are measured repeatedly over time. (e.g. as in a learning study where the same group are observed over a period of time).
Cross-sectional study	Different subjects are measured at different stages of the study (e.g. sampling different people at each stage of learning).

Question 7.12

Design a hypothetical experiment to test the hypothesis that novice users who are given a windows wordprocessor with toolbars and icons disabled will take longer to learn basic word processing tasks than those with the toolbars and icons available.

Answer to 7.12

You need to consider how to operationalise the concepts, specify a set of basic WP tasks, say how you will measure task performance, how will users be selected and allocated to the experimental groups, how many subjects will you use, what statistical test you will use to analyse the results etc.

Examples of areas of usability that have been investigated using an experimental approach include work on learnability based on Carroll et al's concept of minimalist instruction (Carroll 1990). Carroll and his colleagues, in a series of studies in the 1980s, found that time to learn software could be greatly reduced by the use of carefully designed training manuals that provided much less information than traditional manuals and training courses. Kerr & Paynes' (1994) study of the use of animated demonstrations compared with problem solving as methods for learning to use a spreadsheet illustrates the kind of way in which experimentation can be used, as well as revealing some of the shortcomings of the method. They found that users who watched self-running demonstrations of how to use particular software (such as the 'Getting started with Excel' tutorial) performed less well when tested a week later than those who had learned the same package using a text-based problem solving approach. It seemed that the demonstration group had passively watched the demo, without having to perform any mental processing of the information, unlike the problem-solving group. Robson's 'Experiment, Design and Statistics in Psychology' (1973) gives a detailed account of experimental method.

The limitations of the experimental method are its unnaturalness, its inability to take contextual features into account, and its unsuitability at the specification stage. Although not a substitute for the observational approaches described earlier, it can be used to investigate small-scale issues such as the issue of whether or not to use text labels with icons. But one must exercise extreme caution in trying to generalise from the laboratory experiment to any real work situations.

The increasing importance of computer-supported co-operative work environments makes it likely that experimental evaluation techniques will decline in importance. To some extent they suffer from similar disadvantages as the keystroke level modelling approach to analytic evaluation, in that tasks are so split-up and divorced from the real world, making its findings difficult to generalise outside of the laboratory.

Review questions

1. What is meant by usability?
2. Why do we need to analyse user needs before evaluating usability?
3. What are the disadvantages of experimental evaluation?
4. Distinguish between quantitative and qualitative data.

Test questions

1. Evaluate psychological approaches to the measurement of usability

8 The practical evaluation of usability

Introduction

In this chapter we look at ways in which human factors experts and other system designers evaluate the usability of software and systems in practice. Some of the psychologically-based methods discussed in the previous chapter are also used, but we will be concentrating on non-psychological methods here. Topics covered include:

- Heuristics
- Cognitive walkthroughs
- Guidelines
- Observational methods
- Usability labs
- Usability metrics
- Co-operative evaluation
- Surveys

8.1 Expert evaluation methods

Expert evaluation methods don't require testing with end users, and can be applied to a *specification* or a *prototype* rather than needing a full working system. Expert usability specialists assess the interface according to the criteria of the method used- in effect they role-play end-users. Such approaches are cheap because little in the way of resources is required apart from the experts. There are now some software tools to aid in evaluation, for example, EVADIS II which uses a database to analyse responses to questionnaires.

8.2 Heuristic evaluation

Molich and Nielsen (1990) devised heuristic evaluation as a cheap evaluation method for small companies who couldn't afford or hadn't the resources for empirical usability testing. Heuristics are design principles. The expert evaluates the design specification or prototype in terms of the following general heuristics:

- use simple and natural dialogue
- speak the user's language

- minimise user memory load
- be consistent
- provide feedback
- provide clearly marked exits
- provide shortcuts
- provide good error messages
- prevent errors

The expert will evaluate each screen against the list of heuristics, and also the flow of the interaction from one screen to another. This is repeated two or three times and the list of problems aggregated. We looked at the use of heuristics for the design of interfaces in Chapter 6.

Question 8.1

Give a concrete example of each of Molich & Nielsens' 9 heuristics.

An important Question in heuristic evaluation is how many evaluators are required? When the evaluators are both experts in HCI evaluation, and in the particular kind of interface being evaluated, between two and three evaluators will be sufficient to find most of the usability problems. Nielsen found that five evaluators were sufficient to locate three quarters of usability problems.

Heuristics are cheap to implement, don't require end-users and identify a high proportion of usability problems when carried out by a small (2-4) number of evaluators. However, the evaluators need experience of usability.

Question 8.2

How many evaluators are needed for heuristic evaluation?

8.3 Cognitive walkthroughs

In a walkthrough the expert determines the exact task, the context, and important characteristics of the user population, for example:

'You want to use the library photocopier number 4 to make one copy of a journal article and reduce the size so that two pages will fit on one sheet of A4 paper. The user is a second-year student but has never used this particular photocopier before'.

The evaluator then 'walks through' the actions necessary, attempting to predict user behaviour, problems likely to be encountered and strategies used to solve the problem. Results are recorded using a checklist.

Tasks are broken down into goals and sub-goals, and the actions necessary to proceed from one sub-goal to the next. Well-designed interfaces will guide the selection of appropriate actions that lead towards the next sub-goal.

Question 8.3

Attempt a walkthrough for a novice user of your usual word processing package for moving a block of text from page 3 to page 6 of an already open file. Record your results on paper. What problems are users likely to encounter?

Walkthroughs have been found to reveal a high proportion of serious interface problems experienced by users, and are a cheap technique to use.

8.4 Guidelines

Many guidelines exist, from the general to the very specific. At one extreme, Microsoft's Windows Interface Application Design Guide (Microsoft 1992) states 'An application should be visually, conceptually and linguistically clear'. At the other, Smith & Mosier's guidelines contain 944 detailed and commented guidelines with supporting empirical and theoretical material, arranged under the following six categories:

- Data entry
- Data display
- Sequence control
- User guidance
- Data transmission
- Data protection

Question 8.4 What is wrong with the example Microsoft Windows guideline given above?

2.3-1 Consistent format

Adopt a consistent organisation for the location of various display features, insofar as possible, for all displays.

Example: One location might be used consistently for a display title, another area might be reserved for data output by the computer, other areas dedicated to display of control options, instructions, error messages, and user command entry.

Exception: It might be desirable to change display formats in some distinctive way to help a user distinguish one task or activity from another but the displays of any particular type should still be formatted consistently among themselves.

Comment: the objective is to develop display formats that are consistent with accepted usage and existing user habits. Consistent display formats will help establish and preserve user orientation There is no fixed display format that is optimum for all data handling applications, since applications will vary in their requirements. However, once a suitable format has been devised, it should be maintained as a pattern to ensure ,consistent design of other displays.

Example of display guideline from Smith & Mosier (1986)

The Smith & Mosier guidelines are particularly important as they formed the basis for the ISO 9241 standard for software.

Style guides are product-specific guidelines, such as the Open Look, Motif and Apple guidelines, concerned with the application of general principles within the particular environment, for example the use of a 3.5" floppy disk icon for saving a file in Windows applications (an earlier implementation of the save icon in Excel used a pig symbol, on the assumption that Americans associated saving with the savings bank, represented by the piggy-bank icon. The icon was changed as a result of end-user feedback which showed that the association was not made by users in the context of saving an Excel worksheet).

Answer to 8.1	*Use plain language, don't expect users to remember complicated sequences of actions etc.*
Answer to 8.2	*2-5.*
Answer to 8.3	*Depends on the package. Typical problems are users forgetting to select before trying to move the text, not knowing where to find text move commands, confusing cutting with copying etc.*
Answer to 8.4	*The concepts are much too general and vague, compare with the detailed Smith & Mosier guidelines.*

The main problem with the Smith & Mosier guidelines (and some others from the same period) is that they pre-date the widespread availability of graphical **direct-manipulation** (mouse-driven) interfaces such as the Apple Macintosh and Windows interfaces, and therefore place less emphasis on them. Mayhew (1992) attempts to provide a more up-to date set of guidelines, covering the following dialogue styles:

- Command language
- Menus
- Function keys
- Form-fill
- Question and answer
- Natural language
- Direct manipulation

Compared with Smith and Mosier, Mayhew omits the Query language and Graphic selection dialogue styles, while Smith & Mosier omit Direct manipulation.

Question 8.5	**What is the main problem with the Smith & Mosier guidelines?**

8.4.1 Conclusions on guidelines

Guidelines are cheap and can be applied early in the design life-cycle, and don't require end-user testing or even a prototype. However, they have a number of disadvantages:

1. Very general guidelines (such as the 'should be visually clear' type cited above) mean different things to different designers, and are therefore difficult to interpret. On the other hand, detailed ones are only likely to be suitable for specific systems and users.

2. Guidelines often give contradictory advice, and need to be interpreted in context, for example consistency and grouping of related items, such as the File menu operations in Word for Windows 2.0, often results in novice users mis-keying and inadvertently selecting File Open instead of File Save. This results in the display of a dialogue box which is virtually identical to the Save box (consistency), so much so that the confused novice often fails to read the box title and can't understand why they can't save their file. Such design feature are beneficial for experienced

users, but not for novices. One approach to the design of learning materials for novices, the 'Minimalist instruction' approach, goes so far as to recommend the disabling of most software features for learning basic operations.

3. Guidelines don't necessarily deal with all aspects of a particular interface.

4. Guidelines often anticipate problems which in practice are not experienced by end users. Cuomo and Bowen (1994) found that of the problem types predicted by guidelines, only 22% of them actually caused users difficulty.

5. There is no way to predict quantitatively the severity of the problems identified by guidelines, and attempts to meet compliance with one guideline by changing the interface often results in the breach of a different guideline. Yet since we can't predict severity of problem, and such a high proportion of anticipated problems don't cause end users problems, we have no way of knowing whether or not to make such changes.

6. Guidelines are unable to take account of the task context, yet usability should include context-dependent features.

7. Compliance with guidelines doesn't ensure any given level of usability, and is no substitute for usability testing.

Question 8.6	Why isn't consistency always a good thing in an interface?
Question 8.7	How good at predicting usability are guidelines?

8.5 Other approaches combining expert evaluation and user testing

These approaches try to span the divide between theory and practice. Since they require working systems and end-users, they cannot be used as early in design as the methods described above, but they take into account user and context specific factors, and can be implemented quickly and at low cost. Better interface development environments such as Visual Basic are likely to make such approaches more attractive in future.

EVADIS II (Reiterer & Oppermann 1993) represents a computer-supported expert judgement technique based on guidelines derived from ISO 9241, task analysis, user questionnaires, selection of test tasks and the running of an evaluation session. The software is implemented in Clipper on IBM-PC compatible machines under MS-DOS, and essentially is a database of questionnaires, rating scales and comments which are automatically analysed using the software. However, unlike the evaluation methods described above, it requires some real end users, and so cannot be used to evaluate interface specifications. At present there are no evaluation studies of EVADIS II. It represents a combination of end-user testing and expert evaluation. It will be interesting to see if future versions are implemented in a graphical, direct manipulation version of the software rather than the text-based environment currently used.

Discount Usability Engineering (Nielsen 1989) is an attempt to produce a cheap, quantitative approach using a combination of limited end-user testing with expert evaluation. It is based on Heuristics and testing with 3 or more users. It involves the following stages:

They pre-date direct manipulation graphical interfaces.

See the example given earlier of the Save As and Open dialogue boxes in Word for Windows 2.0.

Guidelines discover many potential problems that don't, in practice, cause users a problem, as many as three quarters of predicted problems are false alarms.

1. Expert evaluation of the system using Molich & Nielsens' heuristics checklist; testing with normal, extreme and typical field values for each input field; and execution of a selection of typical user tasks, including those to be tested with real users.

2. Selection of three or more end users.

3. User test at the normal workplace with test tasks. Neither audio or video recording is used, since the aim is to detect 'User Interface Disasters' (situations where the user is unable to proceed without human help or the user experiences annoying, irrational behaviour from the system *as defined by the user*. A UID occurs where two or more typical users encounter such interface problems.) Think-aloud protocols are used (the test subject is asked to talk through the tasks and any comments or problems encountered), with recording using written notes. At the end of the test the user is debriefed, and invited to make suggestions for eliminating UIDs.

4. Problems found during testing are added to the problem list.

5. The problem list is evaluated for new potential UIDs

6. If user testing reveals more new UIDs a new test cycle is started.

7. Otherwise, if no new UIDs are revealed the usability goals have been met and the system is delivered to the users.

Molich (1994) carried out a case study of discount usability evaluation at an insurance company. He claims the system is aimed at those situations where finding 50-90% of UIDs is acceptable, and is best suited to systems for use by casual users rather than those for experienced users or where it is possible to train users. The case study only required a total of 113 hours of the usability specialist's time, and 30 hours of users' time, making it a very cheap evaluation method.

What, according to Discount Usability Engineering, is a UID?

8.6 Conclusions on expert evaluation

There have been three recent attempts to evaluate expert evaluation methods by comparing their predictions with results from usability tests. These studies found that heuristics and walkthroughs found a high proportion of serious problems, and that group walkthroughs gave better results than individual ones. Similarly, heuristic evaluation is best done by several experts. Guidelines performed much worse, either failing to identify problems, or predicting problems when none occurred in user tests.

Question 8.9 Which are the most effective of the three expert evaluation methods?

8.7 Observational methods of evaluation

Observational evaluation may be either laboratory based or carried out in the field (in the work setting). Both forms evaluate performance with end users, and with either prototypes or complete systems.

Typically, **quantitative** data is collected and analysed relating to task *performance*, for example, time to complete a task, number of tasks completed, number of times help consulted etc.

Qualitative data is also collected about *how* users go about performing tasks, their attitudes to the system etc.

Data is collected using a variety of techniques: video and audio recording, software logging, scan converters (which capture user and screen shots and combine them together), think-aloud protocols or pencil and paper field notes. Increasing use is being made of sociological approaches that emphasise the need to collect contextual data, for example ethnography. Currently, much research is concerned with establishing software metrics for quantitative measurement, for example the MUSiC project at the UK National Physical Laboratory, Teddington, Middlesex.. A major issue in observational evaluation is Hawthorne effects, whereby the group being studied are likely to perform at higher than normal performance levels simply as a result of their being observed.

Question 8.10 Distinguish between qualitative and quantitative data.

8.8 Observation in usability laboratories

Nielsen (1994) surveyed 13 usability laboratories and found that they were typically used for end-user testing, were composed of a test room, an observation room and a control room, used one-way glass screens and video recording of tests. 50% used scan converters. Much of the testing is aimed at collecting qualitative data, and optimal cost-benefit results are derived from tests with three to five users for each round of testing.

Usability testing typically involves a measure of **effectiveness**: to what extent are user goals achieved? for example, what proportion of spelling mistakes in a document are identified and corrected. **Efficiency** measures relate the level of effectiveness achieved to a measure of effort, for example, time required to perform the spell check operation.

Satisfaction is measured by rating scales, for example Likert or semantic differential scales, or by measures such as rates of absenteeism or reported health problems. Broader usability goals such as **Learnability** and **Flexibility** can be measured by comparing overall usability measures for different groups of users such as novice and expert users.

Satisfaction of **legislative requirements** and **health and safety** criteria can be evaluated by expert inspection (by copyright lawyers) and by a combination of user satisfaction ratings and conformance testing against a health and safety checklist.

Answer to 8.8	*A situation, experienced by at least two typical users, where the user is unable to proceed without help, or experiences annoying behaviour from the system.*
Answer to 8.9	*Heuristics and cognitive walkthroughs.*
Answer to 8.10	*Quantitative is concerned with measuring task performance, qualitative with how tasks are performed, users attitudes to the system etc.*

8.9 Usability engineering and metrics

Usability engineering is a process whereby product usability is specified quantitatively, in advance. The system or a prototype is then tested to show that it does reach the specified criteria. It consists of the following steps:

- define usability goals through metrics
- set planned levels of usability to be achieved
- analyse the impact of possible design solutions
- incorporate user-derived feedback in product design
- iterate through the design-evaluate-design loop until planned levels are achieved

Usability **metrics** are attempts to establish objective criteria for usability evaluation. Whiteside suggests the following checklist of measures as a starting point for establishing a suitable set of metrics:

Possible measurement criteria

1. Time to complete task.
2. Percentage of task completed.
3. Percentage of task completed per unit time (speed metric).
4. Ratio of successes to failures.
5. Time spent in errors.
6. Percentage number of errors.
7. Percentage or number of competitors that do this better than current product.
8. Number of commands used.
9. Frequency of help or documentation use.
10. Time spent using help or documentation.
11. Percentage of favourable/unfavourable user comments.
12. Number of repetitions of failed commands.
13. Number of runs of successes and of failures.
14. Number of times the interface misleads the user.
15. Number of good and bad features recalled by users.

16. Number of available commands not invoked.

17. Number of regressive behaviours.

18. Number of users preferring Your system.

19. Number of times users need to work around a problem.

20. Number of times the user is disrupted from a work task.

21. Number of times the user loses control of the system.

22. Number of times the user expresses frustration or satisfaction.

The International Standards Organisation ISO 9241 proposes various metrics for usability as follows: (Dix et al 1993)

Usability objective	Effectiveness measure	Efficiency measure	Satisfaction measure
Suitability for the task	Percentage of goals achieved	Time to complete a task	Rating scale for satisfaction
Appropriate for trained users	Number of power features used	Relative efficiency compared with an expert user	Rating scale for satisfaction with power features
Learnability	Percentage of functions learned	Time to learn criterion	Rating scale for ease of learning
Error tolerance	Percentage of errors corrected successfully	Time spent on correcting errors	Rating scale for error handling

Question 8.11

What are usability metrics? Give examples.

The advantages of metrics and usability engineering is that they provide an agreed definition of usability against which an interface or complete system can be measured.

Its disadvantages are the unnaturalness of the laboratory environment and the need for skilled usability engineers. Work in progress at the National Physical Laboratory (NPL), Teddington, on the MUSiC project, has produced a Usability Context Analysis Guide incorporating a context of use Questionnaire and a context report table. Examples of context features recorded include:

- Equipment description, function and specification

- User details, skills and knowledge, age, gender, intellectual and physical capabilities, attitude and motivation

- Task name, goal, frequency and duration, physical and mental demands, task output

- Environment: workplace conditions, design , safety, technical environment, organisational aims, structure and culture, work practices, management structure etc.

Answer to 8.11   *Objective test criteria such as percentage of errors, frequency of use of help, number of occasions users express frustration etc.*

The NPL approach is an expert evaluation of the impact each contextual characteristic is likely to have on usability. Then a decision is made whether each characteristic needs to be controlled, monitored or ignored, for example if lighting level is to be controlled, usability measurement could be carried out with fixed lighting conditions. Manipulation of controlled variables could also be used, for example testing usability on two matched groups but under different lighting conditions. Compared to traditional usability engineering, the NPL/MUSiC approach aims to produce metrics which include contextual information, and an approach to usability engineering that can be used in the field as well as in the laboratory.

8.10 Co-operative evaluation

This approach is a low-cost technique for designers and users without specialist HCI training. It was developed by Monk et al (1993) at York University. The following procedure is adopted:

- Typical users of the product are recruited

- Representative tasks are selected

- Users work with the system attempting the tasks. Verbal (think-aloud) protocols are recorded by evaluators making notes

- Post-test surveys to check users' attitudes and opinions are carried out

- Testers are debriefed

A similar approach to the above, but with the addition of test metrics, is used by PC Magazine UK in their usability lab comparative product tests, although in this case it is finished products that are evaluated rather than prototypes, and the aim is comparative ratings of usability rather than feedback for designers. Each month the magazine carries out comparative usability tests of software.

Question 8.12   Describe briefly a low-cost technique for comparing usability of products.

8.11 Conclusions on observation in usability labs

To a large extent, usability testing is often perceived as the use of one or other of the above techniques in a laboratory setting, as opposed to either observation in the field or experimental study in the lab. This is the definition of usability testing that we shall use here.

Studies indicate that usability testing uncovers most serious and recurring problems, and that it need not be particularly expensive, particularly if 'Discount usability testing' (Molich) is adopted, a technique which combines limited usability testing with expert evaluation.

Usability testing is especially useful to uncover problems of interpretation, and execution errors such as problems double-clicking. Usability testing also provides a baseline against which other types of evaluation can themselves be evaluated. However, usability testing depends on skilled testers and suitable measures of usability (often metrics). It also lacks the ability to fully take account of the context of work.

Question 8.13   How effective is usability testing?

8.12 Observational techniques in the field

Contextual inquiry involves users and evaluators identifying usability issues in the natural work setting, using discussions and interviews to try and reveal the interpretations of their actions that the users place on their behaviour. It doesn't matter whether or not a group of users has an 'incorrect' view of the purpose and result of a particular action, since what guides their behaviour is their understanding of what is happening.

For example, observation of casual users of Excel 4 often reveals that after having produced a chart using the 'chart wizard', users expect to be able to step back through the stages to edit the chart, since this facility is available to them during the chart creation stage. But no such facility is available, leading to frustration for users.

Contextual inquiry is rather like co-operative evaluation, but in the work setting rather than the laboratory. Video and verbal protocol recording is used, rather than metrics.

Question 8.14   How does contextual inquiry compare to co-operative evaluation?

Ethnography describes a wide range of techniques with their origins in Sociology and anthropology which attempt to record as much information as possible about behaviour in context. Video recording is often used, and multiple views of the same situation collected from different users in the same workplace, which can then be compared.

As more systems are designed for co-operative work environments, or for open communications networks, ethnographic techniques are likely to be refined and increasingly important.

Evaluators need to identify the different **stakeholders** (interest groups) in a work environment and their concerns, issues and values. To understand the contexts of an Information System an approach to evaluation is needed which recognises the stakeholders, their motivations, organisational rituals and symbols (e.g. many managers have much more powerful computers than they need, as a mark of their status) and the acknowledgement that many functions are covert (hidden) and that there will often be conflicts between different stakeholders in the organisation. For example, in some situations it is even possible that decisions to purchase a particular system could be taken by someone who has informal links with the system's supplier. Such situations may border on the criminal, but undoubtedly do occur from time to time.

A final field method is **Discount Usability Engineering**, which has already been described above. The technique attempts to apply metrics to usability testing in the field following expert heuristic evaluation.

Answer to 8.12	*Co-operative evaluation or discount usability engineering*
Answer to 8.13	*It uncovers most serious problems, especially problems of users misinterpreting software operation.*
Answer to 8.14	*Contextual inquiry takes place in the work setting, co-operative inquiry in a lab. Co-operative evaluation uses metrics, Contextual Inquiry tries to get at the user's understandings of how the software works.*

8.13 Conclusions on observational methods

Observation of users would appear to be the best way to discover actual usability problems as experienced by users, but data analysis can be difficult and time consuming. A Combination of metrics with ethnographic/contextual techniques appears to offer powerful tools for interface evaluation. Nielsen's 'Discount Usability Engineering' attempts to provide a cheap, practical approach combining metrics, observation in the field and heuristic evaluation.

Question 8.15   Why do ethnographic approaches record the views of many different users?

8.14 Survey-based evaluation

These methods use either interviews or questionnaires, and are useful for obtaining information about subjective aspects of usability such as users' preferences and attitudes towards an interface or feature. But they can also be used to collect background information about factors such as education and experience with computers, and information about the environment and context of use. They are particularly useful for obtaining users' views of the system, and are much used in ethnographic approaches.

Interviews differ from Questionnaires in that they can be less rigidly structured, and allow further probing to suit the context and responses. However, they require trained interviewers and rich, qualitative data can be difficult and time consuming to analyse. However, structured interviews can be used, which are similar to questionnaires and are easier to analyse. They are particularly effective when combined with observation, for example in co-operative evaluation and contextual inquiry (described earlier).

Questionnaires are much less flexible than interviews, but can be used to reach a wider subject group, can be analysed more easily and don't require trained personnel to administer.

Questions can be of several types. Open ended allow the greatest range of response, but are the hardest to analyse. Yet they provide the richest data. Closed and multiple-choice Questions are easy to analyse. Rating scales are particularly useful for recording attitudes and preferences quantitatively, and can be used to set user satisfaction acceptance criteria. Examples of rating scales include Likert scales such as the following:

strongly agree	agree	slightly agree	neutral	slightly disagree	disagree	strongly disagree

Using the Excel 'wizard' to create a chart from your data is easy?

5 to 7 point scales are recommended, rather than 3 or 10 point ones, since very fine-grain scales are difficult to interpret, and very coarse ones don't allow an adequate range of expression.

Since Health and Safety legislation increasingly requires that software be perceived as easy to use, and that workstations meet specific ergonomic requirements, the use of Questionnaires and attitude scales are likely to become increasingly important. ISO 9241-10 requirements cover several dimensions of suitability: for the task, for learning, conformity with user expectations etc.

Can the employee decide in which manner, in which order and with which methods and tools he or she can accomplish his or her tasks?

Answer options: ( ) no   ( ) sometimes   ( )yes

Notes:

---

*How **not** to devise a question: the above is a triple question, and has too coarse a measurement scale*

Question 8.16   Why do attitude scales typically have a 5–7 point scale?

8.15 Conclusions on survey evaluation

The strengths of the methods are their ability to capture the richness of use in context, and to evaluate subjective dimensions of usability. They fit particularly well with ethnographic approaches, but can also be incorporated into observational techniques such as those associated with MUSiC and EVADIS II. Given the increasing legislative requirements to explore and record subjective dimensions of usability (e.g. the UK Display Screen Equipment Regulations EEC 90/270) these methods are likely to assume even greater importance in the future.

8.16 Practical evaluation: a suggested method for those with limited time and money

- Understand the users-find real users

- Understand the tasks-get concrete detailed examples from end users

- Identify representative tasks and produce scenarios for each sample task spelling out what actions users take and what they will see on screen. Discuss the scenarios with some real users

- Copy interaction techniques from other systems that users are familiar with, even if they aren't the most efficient

Answer to 8.15   *Because different users will have their own different goals and motivations in a real work setting, and users' goals often differ from those of managers.*

Answer to 8.16   *Because for example 3 point scales don't give an adequate range of choices, while 9 point scales are difficult to interpret and analyse.*

- Rough-out designs on paper; discard features that don't support any of the required tasks.

- Show paper mock-ups to a few real users.

- Create a prototype, for example in Visual Basic.

- Evaluate **without** users:

    Cognitive Walkthrough e.g. 'You want to use the photocopier to make one copy and reduce from A3 to A4 size'. Gives the best understanding of problems.

    Analytic analysis e.g. KLM, GOMS. Typically 1000 actions for a single 10 minute task. Only appropriate in special cases such as when considering which tasks need keyboard shortcuts.

    Back-of-the envelope analysis: every action takes 2-3 seconds. Much quicker than KLM etc.

    Heuristics: Nielsen & Molich identify the following general heuristics:
    1. Use Simple and natural dialogues
    2. Speak the user's language
    3. Minimise memory load
    4. Be consistent
    5. Provide feedback
    6. Provide shortcuts
    7. provide clearly marked exits
    8. Good error messages
    9. Prevent errors

    Does the software meet all of these? Between 3 and 5 experienced interface experts can identify all major problems and 75% of total identifiable problems using these heuristics

    Guidelines miss many severe problems, but are helpful at the design stage rather than for evaluation

    A Cognitive Walkthrough followed by Heuristics with several evaluators will catch most problems.

- Test with real users and record the tests. Ensure ethical procedures are followed. De-brief the testers.

    o Task **process** data tells us about the hows and whys, use think aloud protocol analysis

    o Task **performance** data tells us how long, how many times etc.

- Iterate (repeat) until specific usability acceptance criteria are met.

- Use interface toolkits and prototyping systems- about 50% of the software code is interface code, e.g. Motif, HyperCard, Visual Basic.

- Design manuals, training packages, on-line help and support using 'minimal manual' approaches.

8.17 Evaluation methods compared: a summary

Evaluation method	Analytic	Expert	Observational	Survey	Experimental
Examples	KLM, GOMS, CCT, CLG, BNF, TAG	Guidelines, Heuristic Evaluation, Cognitive Walkthrough, Discount Usability Evaluation	Can be field or usability-lab based, e.g. Contextual Inquiry, Usability Engineering, metrics	Interviews, Questionnaires, rating scales (e.g. Likert, semantic differential)	Controlled manipulation of variables and hypothesis testing. Statistical analysis.
Interface development life-cycle stage	Specification	Specification or Prototype	Simulation or Prototype	Simulation or Prototype	Normally full Prototype
User involvement	No users, tasks specified and performance criteria established by task analysis	Experts Role-play end-users	Real users, no task restrictions	Real users, no task restrictions	Real users, no task restrictions
Data and information	Quantitative	Qualitative	Qualitative/ quantitative. Video recording, software logging, verbal protocols, 'wizard of oz'.*	Qualitative/ quantitative. Focus on subjective data	Normally quantitative
Advantages	Usable early in design. Few resources required. Cheap. Does not require prototypes or end-users.	Efficient and cheap. Experts not only identify potential problems but suggest solutions. Overview of whole interface. Few resources needed apart from experts, therefore cheap. Detects high proportion of significant problems.	Quickly highlight problems. Verbal protocols a rich source of qualitative data. Can be used for rapid iterative development.	Addresses users' opinions and attitudes towards interface. Can be used on large groups of users. Rating scales can be used to produce easily-analysable quantitative data. Can be used for diagnostic purposes. Can be used with designers.	Good reliability and validity. Quantitative data can be analysed statistically. Can compare different groups.

* Can focus on task (how do users tackle problems) or performance (how long do they take, how many errors/help consultations etc.).

Evaluation method	Analytic	Expert	Observational	Survey	Experimental
Disadvantages	Relies on assumptions about users' actions. Lack of diagnostic output for redesign. Can be difficult to implement since there is limited guidance on how to use methods. Takes no account of learning or error behaviour. Task analysis is no substitute for end-user involvement.	Experts. are likely to have their own biases. Difficult to adopt the role of an end-user.	Observation can affect user behaviour and performance (Hawthorne effects) Data analysis can be difficult and time-consuming.	Possible interviewer bias. Low response rates for postal Questionnaires. Analysis can be complicated and lengthy. Interviews time-consuming.	Needs appropriate laboratory facilities and good knowledge of experimental methods and statistics. Tasks can be artificial and restricted. Cannot always generalise to a real world system. Experimenter bias can be a problem.
Conclusions	Modern development environments such as Visual Basic allow very rapid prototyping.	'Discount Usability Engineering' (Nielsen) an efficient approach. Spans the divide between analytical and observational approaches.	Combination of ethnographic methods such as contextual inquiry with metrics provide a powerful evaluation tool that can be used with end-users and full prototypes.	Likely to become more important given increasing legislative requirements for software to meet user feedback and satisfaction criteria e.g. EEC 90/270	Increasing importance of co-operative work environments and open communications systems make the artificiality of the experiment ever more apparent. Ethnographic approaches represent a major alternative.

Review questions

1. What are metrics?

2. List nine heuristics.

3. Describe the typical usability lab.

4. How could we measure user attitudes to interfaces?

5. When might you use an experiment to evaluate an interface?

Test questions

1. Compare expert and analytic evaluation. In what circumstances would you use each?

2. What evaluation methods would you use for a Computer Supported Co-operative Work (CSCW) environment such as air traffic control?

3. Design a discount usability evaluation for a software package that you are familiar with in order to assess its learnability for new users of the package.

4. How would you compare usability of selecting icons with a mouse from a toolbar compared with using keystrokes to drop down and select from a menu?

9 Designing support materials

9.1 Introduction

This chapter will examine the design of materials such as training courses and manuals, reference material, help and support to enable users to get the most from the system. An important issue is the design of appropriate instructional materials, which is much more complex than might be thought. One has only to glance at the shelves of any computer book shop to see row after row of guides to popular application packages, yet if the documentation with the applications was adequate there would be no need for such guides.

- Issues in the design of support materials
- Minimalist Instruction
- Software documentation standards: BS 7649
- Training materials: animated demonstrations, problem-solving approaches
- Manuals
- Help and on-line support
- Customer support help desks
- Tools to support the design of support materials

9.2 Issues in the design of support materials

The design of support materials is often left to the last stage of development, at which point it is too late to subject such materials to the same user-centred iterative design and evaluation cycle that has been applied to the design of the software. Yet designing support material is just as complex an issue, and needs to be subjected to the same processes of participative user-centred design, evaluation, prototyping and re-design. Useful, functional products that have high levels of usability can still be let down by poorly designed support materials, although the reverse is unlikely to be true – good support materials are unlikely to be able to compensate for a badly designed product.

Anyone who has taught beginners to use a popular application such as a word processing or spreadsheet package, or who has staffed a help desk, will know that users don't read the manuals and don't follow detailed instructions, yet much material is based on the erroneous assumption that they do. We saw in Chapter 6 that on-line support systems often have a special section entitled RTFM (Read The * Manual), and there is at least one series of computing books that contains answers to the most commonly asked questions from users. Yet if a rigorous approach was taken to the development of support materials these shouldn't be necessary. Part of the problem is that those who write the support materials are the programmers who wrote the actual software, which of course they know inside out, so it is difficult for them to put themselves in the place of a newcomer to the system. Another set of problems stem from false assumptions about the logical and rational behaviour of humans, which we looked at in Chapter 2.

9.3 Minimalist instruction

Minimalist instruction is based on studies of how users actually make use of instructional materials such as manuals. The approach originally developed in the US by J. Carroll and colleagues at the IBM Thomas Watson Research Centre, and initially focused on the teaching of word-processing packages (the original studies used Displaywrite) to non-computing expert users.

Previously, most education in the computer industry had been aimed at the needs of computer professionals, already educated to a high level in computer science. But the 1980s saw a large increase in new types of non-expert users with no computer science, programming or electronics background and indeed no interest in learning such topics, rather they were interested in learning how to use computers to perform the task that were relevant to them such as the preparation of letters and documents etc. These new kinds of non-expert users were not interested in ploughing through comprehensive reference manuals for the software, studies showed that such users did not read through the manuals anyway (one study found that only 14% of users read the manual).

These users are task-oriented, requiring knowledge of how to perform the tasks that they are motivated (through work,) to perform. For example, the manuals supplied with packages usually conflict with users' preferred learning styles. The standard approach is a step-by-step sequence covering all aspects of the software followed by drill and practice exercises, rather like the way in which foreign languages were taught in schools 30 years ago! However, observations of users have found that they prefer a problem-solving approach, where they use the software to perform real tasks rather than artificial exercises. Users simply ignore the step-by-step approach and get started anyway, relying on their own judgements. However, such an approach is not what traditional software manuals are designed for, and is a learning strategy that such manuals poorly support.

The essence of the minimalist instruction approach is to design materials that:

- allow an almost immediate start on real tasks

- reduce the verbiage of traditional comprehensive manuals

- anticipate errors that are commonly made and provide support for error recognition and recovery

Typically, learners want to 'Do something now, not learn how to do everything'. Often, they don't understand what it was that they did when following the step-by-step approach. By allowing learners to perform tasks that are meaningful to them, such as producing a letter or memo, we can capitalise on both their understanding of their task, and on their motivation to succeed in the task.

New users tend not to read the manual, but instead to just plunge in and attempt tasks and procedures as soon as they are mentioned in manuals. However, doing this in a step-by-step type manual soon gets the learner hopelessly lost. Chapters in manuals with titles such as 'How to use this book' only make things worse by increasing the amount of verbiage.

The step-by-step approach also tends to assume that learners don't make errors (how could they if they are following the instructions?), but this is totally unrealistic. Learners will make mistakes, and will use their own error recovery strategies regardless of what strategies they are told to adopt, such as switching the computer off and back on again, or keeping sending a file to the printer if it doesn't seem to be printing. Such behaviours can have unfortunate consequences (for example filling up hard disks with Windows .tmp files etc.), but any observer of real users should be able to anticipate such actions and minimise the situations that give rise to them and their consequences. A further point about user errors is that they often provide rich opportunities for learning to take place.

Originally, the minimalist instruction approach used brief summary cards for tasks and sub-tasks, but users of these expressed a desire for a more structured approach in the form of a manual, and so the 'minimal manual' was developed by Carroll and his colleagues.

Minimalist manuals are developed just like software systems, using user involvement at the earliest stages of design, evaluating the manual prototypes with users, then re-designing them, repeating the cycle until acceptance criteria are met. The manual design process should be user-centred and iterative. Early involvement and testing is necessary to identify core tasks and typical user errors.

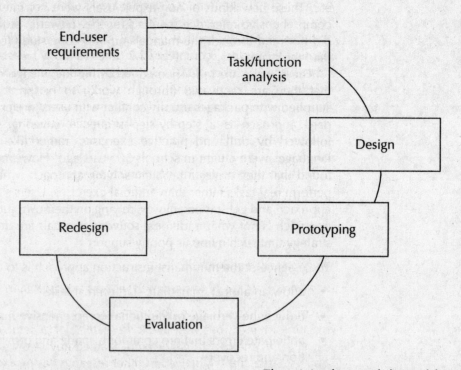

The minimal manual design life-cycle

In the first stage, the focus is on identifying real tasks such as 'Printing documents on paper' rather than system-oriented concepts such as 'The File menu operations'. Minimalist manuals should aim to get the users producing something of their own as early as possible; in the original word processor example the first letter was produced after only seven pages compared with 70 pages in the official manual. Emphasis is also placed on capitalising on users' prior knowledge, such as referring to text block movement procedures as 'cut-and-paste' operations rather than as block movement procedures. Exploratory learning was encouraged with the inclusion of 'try them and see' type exercises, with open-ended exercises at the end of each section of the manual. It is also important to use the vocabulary of the learner such as talking about 'getting rid of blank lines' rather than 'removing extraneous carriage returns'.

Reducing verbiage is vitally important. The minimal manual produced by Carroll was around a quarter the size of the official one, 45 pages compared with 200. Partly this was achieved by avoiding repetition, preview, review, 'welcome to' sections, practice drills and exercises and the index. It was found that trouble-shooting appendices and the index weren't successfully used anyway, and that a better approach was to anticipate errors in the text and deal with error recovery there.

Chapters were organised into short (typically three pages) self-contained task-oriented sections with clear headings, so that the table of contents itself could form an effective index. The language used was simplified and familiar, and user- rather than system-oriented, for example *screen* rather than *visual display unit* etc.

Error recovery was supported by frequent reference to screen displays, forcing users to check that their screen was displaying the correct information.

Once the initial manual was designed, users were observed using the materials and their performance evaluated. Identified problems then lead to a re-design followed by a laboratory based usability evaluation (see chapter six) in a simulated work environment. Two groups of users were given either standard or minimal manuals and observed using them to learn the system and perform a set of work-related tasks. These included standard tasks such as creating, editing, printing, formatting, dealing with headers, footers pagination etc. Users also had access to the official manuals. It was found that minimal manual users spent on average 40% less time learning the system, completed 2.7 times as many tasks and were twice as efficient (a measure of number of tasks divided by time) as the standard manual users. They got started on tasks more quickly and made 20% fewer errors. They also spent much less time using the official manual. The minimal manual users also were much more likely to judge that learning to use the wordprocessor was easy than the standard manual group. The minimal manual took the group the equivalent of one person-month to develop.

In summary, the minimalist manual group:

- took less time
- completed more tasks
- were more efficient
- got started sooner
- were more likely to perceive the tasks as easier than expected.

The minimal manual approach seems to offer impressive improvements in learnability and performance, but we have to be careful of generalising too far from these findings. Carroll and his colleagues only studied novice users of wordprocessors in office settings. Since the original study, other research has shown that the minimalist instruction method also works with European users, and users with different levels of prior computing experience all show gains in performance using the techniques. This is particularly important as more and more users have some prior experience of computing systems, and shows that the gains are just as strong in such circumstances. Interestingly, prior experience of wordprocessors doesn't appear to affect overall learning time.

Below there is a sample page from a 'minimal manual' designed by the author for a popular word-processing package, which illustrates some of the above points on manual design.

Question 9.1   The next page contains a sample minimal manual designed by the author for a beginners course in Word for Windows version 2.0.

Evaluate how far this manual conforms to the principles of minimal manual design outlined above. Note that the original minimal manual idea arose at a time when most packages were still text-based rather than GUI and WIMP based. What difference, if any, do you think this might make?

Question 9.2   Take an application package with which you are familiar, such as a spreadsheet, graphics, DTP etc. package, and design your own minimal manual for new users of the system. Follow the development life-cycle outlined in this chapter.

Starting a new document

As soon as the Word screen appears, you can start typing your text.

Correcting Text

- Type the word *recognise*

- Place the cursor just after the z and press the **backspace** key once(the key to the right of the + and = key).

- Now type the letter s.

- *If the 'e' in recognise disappears when you type the letter s it's because INS is on. On the right of your keyboard there are two INS keys. They act like a switch to turn overtype mode on and off. Press one of the INS keys once only then re-type the missing 'e'.*

- Move to the letter 's' in recognise and press the DEL key. Now type a 'z'.

- Type in the following text; don't press return (enter) at the end of the line. Word wrap will automatically move you onto the next line.

  Carroll and his colleagues have been among the first to recognise that users should develop skills both for doing things (i.e. constructive skills) and for undoing things that have gone wrong (i.e. corrective skills). Being able to detect, diagnose and correct errors is an important skill for all users who need to master a computer program. the provision of error information is therefore a key feature of the Minimalist Manual approach.

  If you get a gap in your text like this:

  Carroll and his colleagues have been

  among the first to recognise that users should develop skills both for doing things (i.e. constructive skills) and

  it is because you accidentally hit return after been. *You can correct this by moving the cursor to just before the a in* among *then pressing the backspace key.*

On your own: Backspace and DEL keys

Go to somewhere in the text you've just typed and practice using the backspace key to delete some text. Now use the DEL key. Can you see the difference between the way they work?

An example page from a 'minimal manual' for a popular wordprocessor

In the above sample page from a minimal manual designed by the author note the way that errors are anticipated, with error information and recovery information in italics. The tasks are based on observation of novice users of the package, whose errors were logged so that recovery information could be incorporated in the manual. The 'On your own' section allows users to practice on real tasks.

9.4 Writing documentation for software

There is a British Standard for the design of software applications documentation: BS 7649, produced in 1993. This goes into some 90 pages of detailed information about documentation design. BS 7649 recommends adopting a life-cycle approach to documentation design, similar to those approaches for systems analysis and design discussed in chapter 5.

BS 7649 recommends the following approach:

- Collect details of users and tasks
- Determine users' documentation needs
- Record users' information needs
- Produce the documentation plan

User information should be collected under the following headings:

- Types of user
- Tasks
- Learning stages
- Environments

9.4.1 Users

The first task is to collect information about users and to group them into user types, with similar characteristics such as experience of computer systems in general, expected knowledge of the application and similar products, and specific language and cultural features, for example a walk-up and use inquiry system for inner-London benefit claimants would have to take account of the potential users whose mother tongue is not English. Lists of users should be produced, grouped into end-users of the system, system support staff, administration staff etc. For example, an order processing system for a textile factory might be used by the sales director, order clerks, sales staff, credit controller, system administrator, production supervisor etc.

9.4.2 Tasks

Having identified groups of users, the typical tasks that they perform should then be drawn up, using the real-world tasks that users perform as the basis. Storyboards can be drawn up of typical task scenarios, using cognitive walkthrough techniques (see Chapter 8). Of course, much of this will already have been done for the software if the recommendations regarding task analysis in Chapter 6 have been followed. For each group of tasks or sub-tasks, establish why they are carried-out, in what sequence, what the pre-requisites are (e.g. check payment before processing order?), how frequently the task is performed, and any necessary sub-tasks.

For example, a task list for an Email system could include the following:

Uses real tasks and user-language, anticipates common errors and shows how to recover from them, encourages exploratory learning etc.

- Access system
- Check if any Email messages are waiting
- Retrieve and read messages
- Reply to messages
- Compose messages
- Address and send messages
- Search for a file
- Retrieve a file
- Send a file

Items on the task list can then be broken-down into sub-tasks (or task hierarchies), for example, sending an Email message can be broken down into:

- Finding the Email address
- Composing the message
- Sending the message
- Updating Email address 'book' where necessary.

Finally, a user-task grid can be drawn-up, showing which users perform which tasks when using the system.

9.4.3 Learning stages

Here we are concerned with the way that users' performance is expected to change over time as they use the system. Stages identified include:

- Before using the system
- First-time use ('Getting Started')
- Normal use
- Advanced use: customisation and shortcuts
- Where appropriate, software installation should also be considered.

It may help to draw up a chart to show which users fall into each of the above stages, in order to identify different training and documentation needs, for example some casual users of the system will never be expected to become advanced users, some tasks may only be performed by advanced users after considerable use of basic system functions etc.

9.4.4 Environments

Environment issues include the following:

- What hardware is available
- Is the environment especially dirty, oily, dusty, humid, hot or cold etc.

- Is there suitable space for paper documentation (for example, a system designed to be used by fire-fighters to analyse gas escapes on laptops has very different environmental requirements from a telephone booking system for a hotel).

Once the information about users, tasks, learning stages and environments has been collected, the next stage is to decide what information each type of user needs. This can be divided into the following types of information:

- Introduction to the system and its features

- Tutorial information on how to perform typical tasks

- Quick reference information

- Comprehensive reference information (the typical thick manual)

- Installation information where appropriate (e.g. support staff who install the software)

It is helpful to relate the different types of information to the learning stages, for example Introductory overview material is only normally needed before using the product and on first use. An example of such an approach is the introduction to Microsoft Access, which allows the user to turn off the screen with the introductory option once they have used it, so that on subsequent use the option is not displayed.

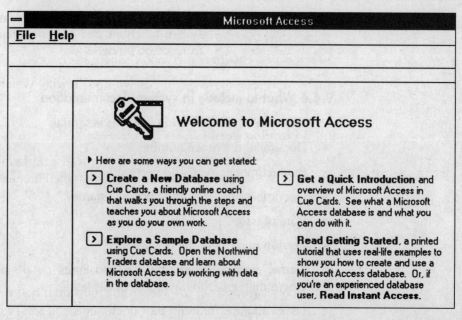

Microsoft Access opening screen

Similarly, quick reference material is used in the normal use and advanced use stages. It is also important to consider *where* users will be using the system in each stage, as this can affect issues such as the availability and storage of different types of documentation. Training may occur in special training rooms with tutorial manuals available, but these may not be available at the normal workplace.

The next stage is to record the information requirements for each type of user at each of the learning stages, taking environmental factors into account at each stage.

Finally, a documentation plan can be produced to identify what information is to be provided to each type of user, at each learning stage, in what form (on-line, paper, video, multimedia training package etc.)

9.4.5 Document types and their use

Book	Reference and tutorial material
Card	Useful for small amounts of quick reference information
Wall chart	Useful for large amounts of quick reference information (e.g. descriptions of spreadsheet functions)
Keyboard templates	Only suitable if the user is using just one application, such as a wordprocessor operator
Post-it note stuck on the computer	Useful for small amounts of information and for information about customised features such as macros
On-line help	Suitable for quick reference material, but should not normally exceed one screen full of information. Not suitable for tutorial information. Navigation through help topics can be very difficult as you can't predict topics that users will need help with.
Booklets	Suitable for getting started type material with an overview of the system functions and screens, often in an A4 lie-flat booklet using comb binders.

9.4.6 What to include in system documentation

BS 7649 regards the following items as essential:

- Document reference number
- Product model, type and version
- Document title, including product name
- Date of issue
- Version number of the document
- Name, address, telephone, fax and Email details of the product supplier and, where different, the document publisher
- List of all parts for multi-part documents and sets of manuals

Where appropriate, documents should contain:

- ISBN number
- Copyright statement
- Author details
- All documents except quick reference documents should contain contents lists, and indexes and a glossary where appropriate.
- Copyright and licensing terms conditions
- Warranty and support information and procedures

- Statement of consumer rights, training and related assistance, source code availability

- Software information to be included:

- Software name and code, version, date and manufacturer

- Components supplied and associated optional products which may be relevant

- Software purpose and functions

- Environments for which software is designed, including hardware and software requirements

- Performance characteristics

- Restrictions and security facilities

- Details of any other documents, such as DOS or Windows manuals, that users are expected to have available

9.4.7 General points on documentation writing style

- Use a simple style, but don't patronise.

- Divide text into short sections with clear section headings and appropriate use of white space. Jokes should be avoided. Humour and cartoons may be appropriate

- Complex ideas should be broken-down into simpler components

- Warnings should be given in the imperative-Stop!

- Illustrations, lists and tables should be used where they better convey ideas than text, or help to clarify the text. They also help to break-up the text.

Question 9.3

Design a documentation plan for a new budget windows word processor aimed at home and small business users

9.4.8 Contents of introductory material

These should aim to help the user decide whether the software is suitable for the task, including brief details of how to use the software and illustrations of screens. Paragraphs should be short, preferably no more than six lines.

- Section headings should be short and clear.

- Sections should be very short, no more than two pages

- There should be one main section for each major topic

- There should be no cross-references, appendices, index or glossary

Answer 9.3

Points to consider are that it is likely to be less fully-featured than products such as Wordperfect or Word, that many users will be novices, that appropriate context sensitive help will be needed etc.

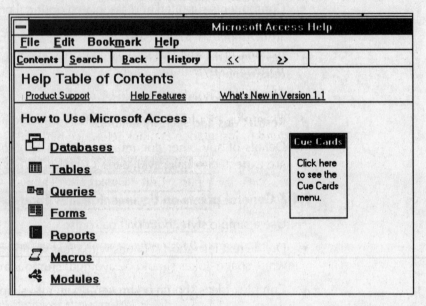

Microsoft Access Help Table of Contents: how to organise material

9.4.9 Installation instructions

Users should be able to follow the instructions in detail.

Instructions should be drafted by someone who has installed the software and written down each step, including possible sources of error or ambiguity. Details of configuring printers and other peripherals should be included.

Instructions should cover backing-up both software and data

9.4.10 Contents of tutorials

The section in this chapter on minimalist instruction is relevant to tutorial production.

- Such documentation should cover starting, quitting from, saving, printing, entering data and other basic functions of the system, based on task analysis and frequency counts of users wherever possible.

- Tutorials should not assume that users follow instructions to the letter. They should also predict likely sources of error and include meaningful error recovery information. Strategies for avoiding errors should also be given.

- Instructions should be given in numbered lists, with each list item requiring the user to perform only one action. Wherever possible, each item should start with a verb, such as Press, Click, Select etc. Each instruction should briefly describe the effect the user should see on screen

- Worked examples should be provided, but they should be carefully chosen to be representative

- Each task section should be designed so that users can complete it in no more than 10 minutes

- Each section should start with an overview, and end with a summary
- Topics should be grouped either by order of use, or by order of grouping in the software, e.g. by menus.

9.4.11 Quick reference materials

- These should state action goals followed by procedure ('To turn highlighted text from upper to lower case......Press CTRL-F3') rather than listing keystrokes or actions first, since users want to do something, not find out what pressing a particular key will do.
- Short, clear headings should be used.
- Examples should be chosen carefully and should be representative, since users tend to just glance at quick reference material.

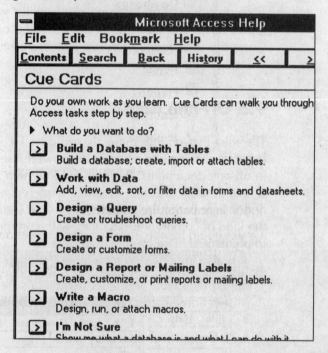

Microsoft Cue cards: an example of quick reference material

9.4.12 Comprehensive reference materials

These won't be used sequentially, so cross-references should be given.

- Topics should be based either on user tasks, or on product divisions such as items on a menu
- There should be a section for each task or product division, preferably starting on a new page There should be an Index and possibly a glossary of terms
- There should be a consistent section numbering strategy
- Diagrams and line drawings are preferable to photographs. graphs and charts are useful for showing general trends and differences
- When designing support materials it is important not to see them as a substitute for a well-designed interface. Manuals, reference cards etc. should be there as a back up rather than as a default.

9.4.13 Designing indexes

A major problem for designers is that there are so many different names for the same operation, such as quit and exit as commands to leave a program. Carrying out a survey of what users call a particular option may tell you what a a majority of users call that option, but a user chosen at random would still have a 50% chance of calling it something else. The moral of this is that there is no correct name for a command, but if you carry out a survey of users and include the five most common synonyms in the index, you will cover around 80% of users. Another implication is that menu-based interfaces that rely on recognition will be better than command interfaces that rely on recall, since it is much easier to recognise that the Exit option on a menu is the command to leave ('Quit') a program. A survey of as few as 10 users will help enormously in choosing appropriate synonyms.

Question 9.4

Take an application that you are familiar with and design an index of Help topics for it. Test your index out on some occasional users of the system. Compare your index with the system's own index

9.5 On-line help

The idea that on-line manuals could replace paper manuals has not been realised, even after taking into account the powerful search and hypertext-like linking possible in on-line documents. Basically on-line help should be limited to brief less-than one screen descriptions such as function references. The problems of what name to use for options are particularly acute for on-line systems, due to space limitations, although the kind of comprehensive index with common synonyms described above could be implemented in an on-line help system.

It is also important to remember that there are problems of navigation with hyper-media systems, so users can easily get lost in a poorly designed system.

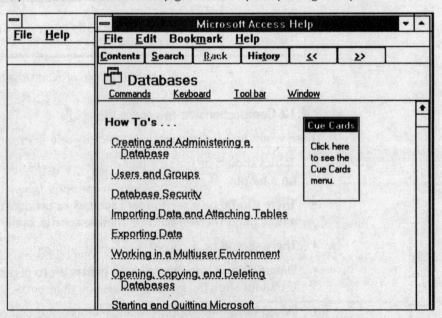

The Microsoft Access help opening screen

9.5.1 Context-sensitive help

A general help system takes no account of where the user is in the software, but a context-sensitive system tailors the help displayed to the mode that the software is in (e.g. design mode rather than data sheet mode for a database system) and the actions that the user has just (or is about to) perform. Such systems typically use the F1 function key and are linked to menus. They avoid some of the problems of indexing discussed above because in a well designed system the context sensitive help will relate to the actions being performed, but only if the user is in the right mode or menu. Such systems are good at explaining the currently available options, but are of little help if the user is in the wrong mode or menu, for example a Word for Windows expert user who wants to preview a document they are working on in WordPerfect for Windows who selects context-sensitive help when in the File menu (where the preview option is located in Word) won't find any advice on how to preview their document in WordPerfect. In such circumstances context-sensitive help is of little use to the user.

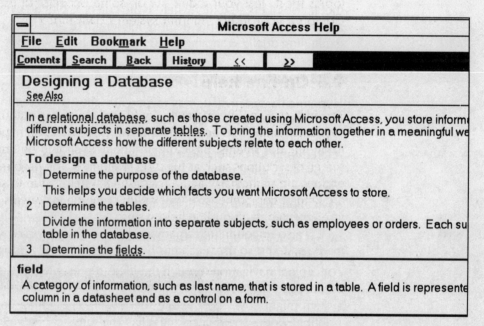

Example of context-sensitive help screen with pop-up hypermedia screen for the item 'fields'.

Balloon help

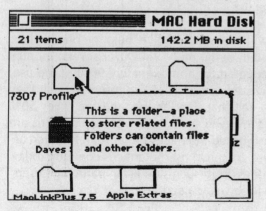

In the Apple Macintosh System 7 balloon help is a form of context sensitive help that displays a text 'balloon' rather like the speech balloons in cartoons, whenever the cursor is placed over a screen object such as a menu label. More experienced users can turn the balloon help option off. In WordPerfect for Windows the top line of the screen displays a brief explanation when the cursor is placed over a menu. Other Windows packages display brief explanations at the bottom of the screen.

Balloon help on the Apple Macintosh

Question 9.5

Is balloon help a good idea? Find some users, both novice and experienced, and find out what they think.

Question 9.6

Examine examples of each of the above mentioned types of automatic context-sensitive help; that where it is displayed at the bottom of the screen, the top of the screen and balloon help. Which do you think is the better system? Carry out a brief evaluation of the three different approaches using some typical end-users and record your results.

9.5.2 'Intelligent' help systems: Intellisense

Some programs such as Word for Windows 6 offers 'Intellisense', a help system that, for example, automatically corrects common mistakes such as typing hte instead of the. It also offers a facility where if the cursor is placed over a menu or menu item but no action occurs for a pre-determined length of time (e.g. 30 seconds) a help message explaining briefly what the menu item does is displayed.

9.5.3 Hypermedia and hypertext help systems

Hypermedia systems such as Hypercard allow the creation of on-screen card-index like 'cards' that can usually store diagrams and pictures as well as text. Some can even include sound clips and animation. Hypertext systems allow the user to link to related topics by selecting a link topic, button or icon, giving the user the option to choose how they want to navigate through the hypertext system. Such systems are ideal for on-line help systems since they allow easy browsing and user-controlled navigation, but because of the choice of navigation are unsuitable for tutorial-type material since their is no way to make sure that all particular topics have been visited by the user. They are however ideal for quick reference type information.

Design of hypermedia systems must deal with two problems: firstly the problem of conceptual navigation through the ideas represented in the system, and secondly the actual physical navigation through the system. For example, an on-line manual for a system might cover conceptual ideas such as opening and closing files, saving and printing work, spell checking etc. The physical navigation issue could use the metaphor of page or chapter numbers and a table of contents. An important task for designers of hypermedia systems is to find metaphors for users' conceptual models of their tasks.

9.5.4 Issues in on-line help design

Typically, around 10% of interactions with systems involve help of one sort or another. A study of an IBM mainframe system in the mid-1980s over several months found that 10% of the help messages accounted for approximately 90% of the use, 15% of the help messages were never accessed, and that 35% of users felt that they had been given helpful information, 15% felt that they hadn't, and the other 50% weren't sure whether they had or hadn't. However, such studies of help systems are problematic because they are based on text-based interfaces rather than the increasingly common and supposedly easier to use graphical user interfaces common today. Nevertheless, there are some relevant findings from such studies. In particular, users' help requests typically fall into one of the following categories:

- How do I perform a particular task?

- What does this option do?

- What can I do with this application (or sub-part of it, such as charting in spread-sheet packages)?

- How did that happen? (e.g. when some highlighted text disappears, or part of a sentence appears on a new line)

- How can I fix or undo what I've just accidentally done?

- Whereabouts in the system am I? (for example, confusion between worksheet and charting modes of a spreadsheet, or design and view modes of a database package).

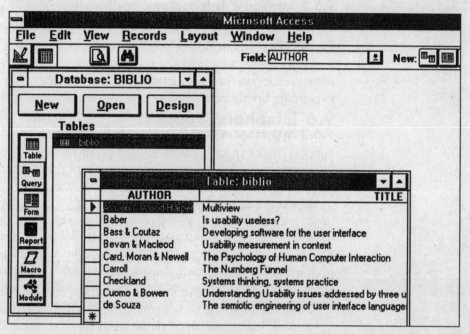

Typical Access screen showing multiple windows. With several different windows and a design and datasheet mode there is a lot of potential for confusion on the part of the user.

Question 9.7

Which of the above typical user questions do the following kinds of help material try to answer? (It would be helpful if you could actually use each type before answering).

1. Animated demonstrations such as the Microsoft 'Getting started' on-screen tutorials

2. Cue cards

3. Wizards

4. Intellisense

5. Hypercard help

6. Balloon help

Question 9.8

Which, if any, of the typical user types of help request are especially difficult to deal with by on-line help systems?

Answer 9.5

One drawback that more experienced users are likely to report is the amount of screen that is obscured by the balloons. Such users often turn balloon help off. Clearly, if you design a similar system you need to consider an option to turn it off.

Answer 9.7

1. *Animated demonstrations-what can I do type questions.*
2. *Cue cards-how to questions*
3. *Wizards-same as number 2*
4. *Intellisense-what does this do type questions*
5. *HyperCard help-task and reference type questions*
6. *Balloon help-same as number 4*

Answer 9.8

Such systems are often poor at the 'how did that happen', 'where am I' and 'how do I get out of this' type questions

9.6 Telephone support

Support lines can be a useful source of information for developers about aspects of the interface to improve in the next version of the software. It can be useful for developers to spend some time manning support lines.

Support staff need to pay particular attention to the heuristic 'Speak the user's language' (Molich & Nielsen). Needless to say, the user shouldn't be made to feel uncomfortable about phoning with their problem. They should also be given enough information so that they can get back to the original person who dealt with their problem rather than having to explain everything again from scratch. Requests for the software registration number are reasonable, but the user should be told just where to find this, and it shouldn't be located on the packaging in case it is inadvertently thrown away.

9.7 Support on the Internet

Many hardware and software vendors provide support on the Internet, through Usenet Newsgroups or through Compuserve forums. Currently there are over 500 forums on Compuserve alone providing support, from companies such as IBM, Microsoft, Apple, Intel, Lotus etc. Currently, it is reasonable to assume that any user using such help is likely to be fairly experienced in computer use, although not necessarily in the particular product. Requests for assistance from users are left in the form of an Email message, which the forum or newsgroup replies to by Email. Once such a service is provided, it can be used by developers to analyse the kinds of problems users are having and to provide a 'frequently asked questions' section in the newsgroup or forum, as well as providing important data for the next upgrade of the system!

9.8 Animated demonstrations for learning applications

Modern application packages make much use of on-screen self-running tutorials to show new users how to use software, but are such approaches effective compared with text manuals or animated demonstrations combined with spoken text?

Immediately after watching such animated demonstrations, users were 50% faster at training tasks than text-only users. However, one week later, the text users performed the same tasks more quickly, suggesting that animated demonstrations encourage a passive approach to the material which is quickly forgotten, whereas users of text manuals have to take a more active learning approach which seems to aid memory retention and also the ability to perform similar (but not the same) tasks later.

Such results suggest that where there is a need for users to quickly learn a system, but no requirement for them to retain that learning, such as in one-off walk up and use type systems, then animated demonstrations are appropriate. But if users are required to retain knowledge and to apply it to conceptually similar tasks, then animated demonstrations may not be suitable. Demonstrations are, however, suited to giving users an idea of the look and feel of the interface and the range of system functions available. It has also been found that users like animated demonstrations and prefer them to text manuals, despite the apparent lack of effectiveness.

Surprisingly, the use of animated demonstrations with spoken text produced no difference in performance compared with the demonstration without text, again suggesting that the passive nature of the learning situation is the key factor leading to reduced levels of performance in the longer term. Such results suggest that users simply mimic or copy what they see in the demonstrations rather than internalising the concepts and procedures.

9.9 Designing support materials for the older user

We saw in chapter two that older users of computers are likely to become more important as the average age of the population increases in most industrialised societies. Support materials for such users should take account of the decline of short-term memory with age, the widespread fear of technology that many elderly people exhibit, the tendency of older users to read screens and documentation more thoroughly rather than just plunging in, and possible difficulties using mice as a result of a decline in manual dexterity with age. Nevertheless, it is important to avoid stereotyping all older users, and to consider each as an individual.

9.10 The use of full-motion video in training materials

With the increasingly widespread availability of multimedia systems it is now feasible to use full-motion video for training computer users.

Full motion video is defined as 15-30 frames per second (fps), with television typically using between 25-30 fps. Below 15 fps the animation is too jerky to be perceived as full motion.

Full motion video may be full-screen, or part-screen, typically quarter-screen, with a proportionate reduction in memory and processing requirements.

A CD-ROM could contain all of the following data:

- 20 min of full-screen 30fps full-motion video

- 80 min of quarter screen 15 fps full motion video
- 10 hours of AM radio quality audio (for speech)
- 2,000 still images
- 5 Megabytes of text and graphics

Studies of full-motion video have found that compared to slide show based systems (where the screen image is updated only every few seconds with still images), full motion video systems lead to improved recall since they offer more realistic learning environments.

9.11 Guidelines for use of full motion video

- Where only some information can be presented in full motion video, use it for the most important points
- Frame rates of 15-30 frames per second (fps) are equally effective
- Full motion video improves the learner's opinion of the learning material compared to slide show based material.

Review questions

1. What special factors need to be considered when designing for older users?

2. Describe the advantages and disadvantages of animated demonstrations and moving video training materials.

3. What are the main features of the minimal manual approach? How successful is it?

4. What are the main factors to consider in the design of documentation?

6. What factors need to be considered in the design of help systems?

7. At what stage in the life-cycle should you start documentation design?

Test questions

1. Choose a package that you are familiar with and design a minimal manual for the package. Test out the manual on some typical users and evaluate your design.

2. Evaluate the use of multi media in software documentation.

3. What are the main types of problems experienced by users? How can help systems best deal with each type of problem?

4. Should documentation designers assume error-free performance by end users? What are the implications of your answer for the design of support materials?

10 Putting it all together: the interface design process

Introduction

In this chapter, we draw together and summarise the earlier chapters.

10.1 Increasing importance of Human Computer Interaction (HCI)

HCI is bound to become more important over the next few years as it is likely to become a legal requirement, under European Union health and safety at work directives, that software is easy to use and provides adequate feedback to users.

HCI will be increasingly important in the following areas:

- as part of the software development process and systems design methods

- as part of future legal requirements for software

- as the basis for a set of usability criteria to evaluate and choose from amongst competing products

- as the basis for a successful marketing strategy to the increasingly important home and small business user

Usability is the term used to describe the practical implementation of HCI goals. The International Standards Organisation define usability as:

> 'the degree to which specific users can achieve specific goals within a particular environment; effectively, efficiently, comfortably, and in an acceptable manner.' (Booth 1989 p110).

10.2 Users

We can divide users of any computer system into the following broad categories:

- **Expert users.** People with in-depth knowledge of the system who use it virtually all the time. They are not necessarily computer specialists, but know the system inside out. For example, an experienced secretary who had been using the same wordprocessor for five years.

- **Novice users.** We are all in this category at some stage. Those who haven't used the system at all before, or only very superficially. For example, computing students who haven't used a particular package before.

- **Occasional users** – the vast majority of us. Such users often use a system quite regularly, but only for a limited range of tasks. Occasional users can be like experts for that range of tasks, but like novices for all other tasks.

- **Users with special needs.** Many users with severe disabilities successfully use computer systems that have been specially adapted, for example blind users can use speech recognition and speech synthesis to enable them to use computers.

10.3 Organisational factors

Most organisations are characterised by different interest groups in conflict with each other. There is a need to analyse the perceived interests of such 'stakeholders' in the organisation. Employees experience of computerisation and changes to the economy and society during the 1970s and 80s has been one of high levels of system failure, with up to 80% of systems producing either no or only marginal benefits; large-scale job losses amongst employees in sectors such as banking and insurance as a direct result of computerisation.

10.4 Analysing user tasks

Before we can design usable systems, we need to know what tasks the software will be used for.

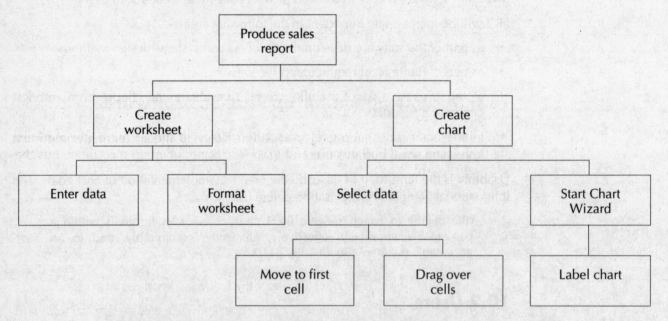

Example of task decomposition chart for producing projected sales report using Excel (from Chapter 7)

10.5 Software ergonomics

Software ergonomics requirements of the UK Display Screen Equipment Regulations 1993, the main health & safety legislation covering computer use.

- Software must be suitable for the task, allowing users to complete tasks efficiently without presenting unnecessary problems or obstacles.

- Easy to use. The software should be easy to learn, intuitive, and appropriate to the user's ability.

- The system's speed of response to commands and instructions should be immediately shown on screen, and should be appropriate to the task and the worker's abilities.

- Adaptable to the operator's skill level. Experienced users should be able to adapt the interface to suit their particular ability level and preferences.

- The software should prevent users from errors and allow error recovery.

- No quantitative or qualitative testing, such as measuring output speed, should be carried out without the operator being informed that such testing is taking place.

- Systems must give VDU workers feedback on their performance. Such feedback should be in an appropriate style and format, and should not contain unnecessary information. Help facilities should be provided.

ISO 9241, the international standard for software design, identifies the following seven principles for dialogue design:

1. Suitability for the task
2. Self-descriptiveness
3. Controllability
4. Conformity with user expectations
5. Error tolerance
6. Suitability for individualization
7. Suitability for learning.

10.6 Documentation for applications software.

BS 7649 recommends that the documentation life-cycle should mirror the software life-cycle, and should be iterative and make use of prototyping. It recommends the following stages:

- Collect details of users and tasks
- Determine users' documentation needs
- Record users' information needs
- Produce the documentation plan

User information should be collected under the following headings:

- Types of user: level of computing experience, knowledge of system, cultural and linguistic factors etc.

- Tasks: make a list of the typical tasks that real users perform, then construct Storyboards of typical task scenarios, using cognitive walkthrough techniques (see chapter six.)

- Learning stages: the way that users' performance is expected to change over time as they use the system.

- Environments: what hardware is available, is the environment especially dirty, oily, dusty, humid, hot or cold etc., is there suitable space for software manuals etc.

BS 7649 regards the following items as essential for all software:

- Document reference number
- Product model, type and version
- Document title, including product name
- Date of issue
- Version number of the document
- Name, address, telephone, fax and Email details of the product supplier and, where different, the document publisher

10.7 Training and support materials

Users don't want to read manuals, and evidence suggests that they don't read them until they get stuck. It's best to acknowledge that users prefer to get going without reading the manual, and to adopt an approach to manual writing based on the minimalist instructional techniques (see chapter seven).

Computerised demonstrations and 'tutorials'

Because of their passive nature, users are unlikely to remember many of the procedures described in such demonstrations. They are however useful for giving the user a quick guide to the interface. If users are only required to retain information on how to use the system long enough to perform a single task, then such approaches can be useful, but they are not suitable for those who have to learn the system for regular use.

Help and reference information

Printed command and action references, with examples, are generally a good idea, especially for those familiar with similar software. There should be cross-referencing since many actions are given different names by different users. Research has shown that if you list a particular operation under the five most common terms used to describe it, over 80% of users will be able to find it under one or other of those terms.

- **Manuals** are only likely to be turned to when users get stuck, rather than when learning the system. There should be several different types of manual, for example a 'Getting started' introduction, tutorial manuals, quick reference information and comprehensive reference manuals.

- **On-line help** is also used when users get stuck, and to look up the syntax for particular actions. The facility to obtain print-outs of selected help topics is very useful. Keep on-line help screens brief: a paragraph rather than a screen full.

10.8 Customer support telephone helplines

Such support helplines can be a useful source of feedback from users concerning usability issues. Make the system developers staff the helplines!

On-line forums on Compuserve, the Internet etc.

At the moment, it is reasonable to assume that any user using such help is likely to be fairly experienced in computer use, although not necessarily in the particular product. Once such a service is provided, it can be used by developers to analyse the kinds of problems users are having and to provide a 'frequently asked questions' section in the newsgroup or forum, as well as providing important data for the next upgrade of the system!

10.9 Legal issues in software design

- There is no need to do anything to claim copyright under the Copyright, Designs & patent Act 1988, it is automatic. However, in the event of a dispute, you may need to prove when you produced the software. Deposit a copy of your software with a solicitor or other independent person.

- Software designers should ensure as far as possible that they are not infringing anyone else's copyright. Pay careful attention to the licensing terms of any clip art, sound and media clips. Multimedia authoring tools in particular often have quite complex rules regarding the distribution of run-time versions with software.

- Licensing terms should be clearly thought out.

- Employees should clarify who owns copyright in any software they produce, themselves or their employer.

- Clarify if the customer or developer owns copyright in the software.

- Systems need to comply with the Display Screen Equipment Regulations 1992 (EEC 90/270)

- Systems storing data about identifiable living individuals must be registered with the Data Protection Registrar.

10.10 Measuring context of use

The UK National Physical Laboratory uses a detailed questionnaire which breaks context of use down into the following categories:

- Equipment: application area and functions, hardware and software. Includes a basic description of the product and its intended use.

- Users: skills, knowledge and personal attributes e.g. age, gender, attitude and motivation, intellectual abilities, product and task experience, level of experience.

- Task: goals, frequency, duration, physical and mental demands, risks as a result of errors.

- Environment: working conditions, organisational attitudes and culture, health and safety factors, job design, payment systems etc.

10.11 Input and output considerations

Keyboards

Keyboards are easy to use and flexible for text and numeric input. Evidence suggests that for most text-entry tasks standard non-membrane Qwerty keyboards with full-travel 'click' keys are the preferred option. Keyboards which don't provide feedback typically reduce typing speed by 20% and double error rates, with not surprisingly lower levels of user satisfaction being reported for such non-feedback keyboards.

Group input: Videoconferencing systems

Videoconferencing systems typically allow several users to share a screen 'white-board' or notebook which they can all access, and to see moving video images of other conference participants on their screen simultaneously.

Speech recognition

Speech recognition systems fall broadly into two groups: **control** systems which allow users to speak commands such as 'save file', 'delete this line', 'go back two pages' etc., and **dictation** systems, which allow recognition and processing of normal every day continuous speech. At present, speech input is mainly targeted at specific vertical markets such as radiologists.

10.12 Interaction styles

These can be broadly classified into command language, menu-based, direct manipulation, natural language, question-and-answer and form-fill. Menu-based styles are generally the most flexible, and can be combined with other styles, for example the Microsoft Access interface combines menus with direct manipulation drag-and-drop actions, form-fill for 'wizards', and command-language for keystroke shortcuts.

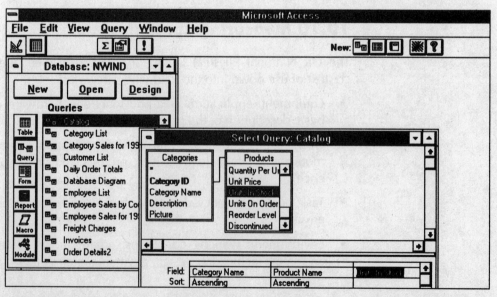

Microsoft Access screen showing multiple windows, menus, and direct manipulation screen objects. Fields from the table can be dragged and dropped onto the query window.

10.13 Problems with traditional systems design methods

Around 30-40% of computer projects are massively over budget, over time and fail to do the job they were supposed to do. Of the remainder, around half deliver only marginal benefits.

The single major source of errors is the requirements stage, where almost 60% of errors occur, followed by the design stage, with around 25%, and coding, responsible for 7%.

Current design practice is to devote the majority of time to the physical design, coding and testing stages, responsible for around 60% of time, with only around 10% devoted to requirements gathering and 15% to logical design.

However, most errors occur in the earliest stages of the life-cycle (around 85% of errors in the first two stages) yet only around 25% of time and resources are devoted to these areas.

From the point of view of interface design, traditional structured analysis methods have little or nothing to say, since in this period systems were always large-scale and text based, with no possibilities of direct manipulation graphical user interfaces.

10.14 Summary of interface design in SSADM version 4

The current version of SSADM, the official UK government systems analysis and design method, takes account of interface design issues.

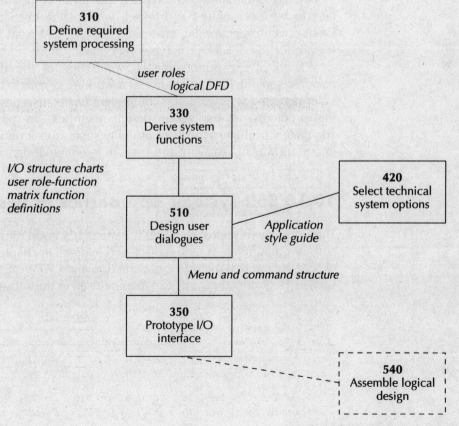

Interface design stages in SSADM 4

10.15 Recent approaches to systems development

Iterative design and prototyping

The iterative approach to systems design involves going back to previous stages a number of times, since we are likely to discover information that requires us to revise the assumptions made in previous stages. The only way we can be really certain about an interface is to build it, test it out on some typical users, then re-design the interface and so-on until our acceptance criteria are met.

Prototypes implement a limited range of the systems features and functions, for example we could design an opening screen with menus and ask users to evaluate the screen design without our prototype screen actually doing anything. A prototype can be anything from a pencil and paper sketch of a screen to a cut-down version of the final product.

A prototype can be throw-away, or it can be evolutionary, where it is used as the basis for the next interface design. However, we can't assess all aspects of usability from prototypes. In particular, they can't be used to assess features such as task performance times and reliability.

Types of prototyping

Storyboards are **non-working** screens that can be evaluated by users in terms of features such as language, screen messages, screen layout and use of colour etc.

A set of such non-functioning screen designs can be turned into an animated demonstration to provide an idea of the sequence of screens displayed to the user, using an authoring or presentation package.

Limited-functionality prototypes allow some of the interactive nature of the interface to be incorporated and tested, without the need to build complete systems. Event-driven programming environments such as Visual Basic and HyperCard make the production of such prototypes very quick.

Wizard of Oz prototyping is where one of the designers fakes appropriate responses, giving the appearance of a working system to the user.

Prototyping is an essential component of iterative design, but it can't solve all of the problems of traditional design methods. In particular, prototyping can't adequately evaluate aspects of usability such as task performance. However, it is an important way of involving end-users in interface design at the earliest stages.

10.16 Soft-systems approaches to design

The soft-systems approach (SSM) is particularly good for gathering information about end-user requirements, and is discussed in detail in chapter five. The most useful parts of SSM are the rich picture, root definition and CATWOE tests. Traditional techniques such as Data flow diagrams can then be used in the subsequent stages.

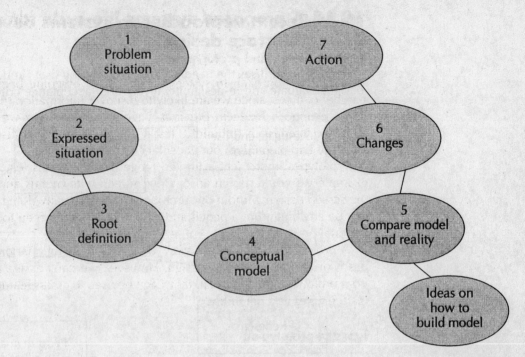

The stages of SSM

10.17 The Star Model of the system life-cycle

Most approaches to systems design still use a 'stage' model, albeit with the addition of iteration and prototyping. However, the star model is based on the principle that systems analysis and design can start at any stage and doesn't have to follow a particular progression, with development proceeding simultaneously in both a top-down and bottom-up fashion. Evaluation is placed at the centre of the model, to emphasise its importance, compared with the testing stage in traditional design methods.

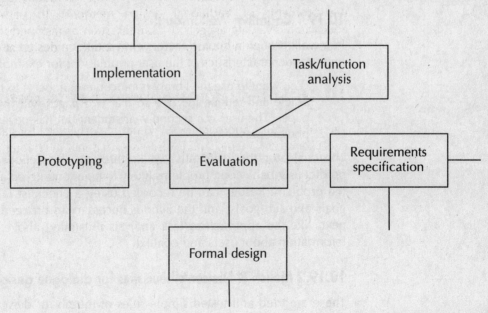

The Star Life-cycle

10.18 A proposed systems life-cycle for systems interface design

This model prioritises the need to start off analysing users and their tasks, and to then design, evaluate and re-design iteratively until acceptance criteria are met.

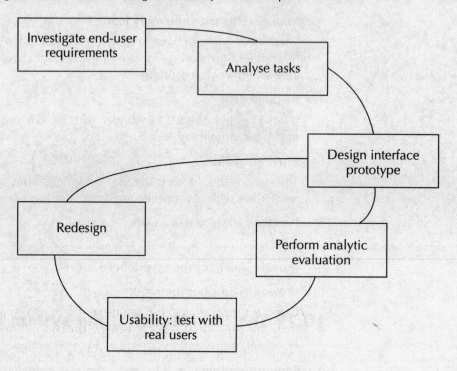

10.19 Evaluating designs: guidelines, heuristics, walkthroughs

10.19.1 Cognitive Walkthrough

In a walkthrough a human factors expert determines the exact task, the context, and important characteristics of the user population; for example:

> 'You want to use the library photocopier number 4 to make one copy of an article and reduce the size so that two pages will fit on one sheet of A4 paper. The user is a second-year student but has never used this particular photocopier before.'

The evaluator then mentally 'walks through' the actions necessary, attempting to predict user behaviour, problems likely to be encountered and strategies used to solve the problem. Results can be recorded using a checklist. Tasks are broken down into goals and sub-goals, and the actions necessary to proceed from one sub-goal to the next, like the approach to task analysis illustrated above, but with the addition of information about users and context.

10.19.2 Molich & Nielsen's heuristics for dialogue design

These are tried and tested simple rules of thumb for design that have actually been shown to work in several studies (see chapter six).

1. **Use simple and natural dialogue**

   All information should appear in a natural and logical order.

2. **Speak the user's language**

   The dialogue should be expressed clearly in words, phrases and concepts familiar to the user rather than in system-oriented terms.

3. **Minimise the user's memory load**

   The user should not have to remember information from one part of the dialogue to another. Instructions for use of the system should be visible or easily retrievable whenever appropriate.

4. **Be consistent**

   Users should not have to wonder whether different words, situations or actions mean the same thing.

5. **Provide feedback**

   The system should keep the user informed about what is going on by providing him or her with appropriate feedback within a reasonable time.

6. **Provide clearly marked exits**

   There should always be an 'Exit' option clearly available.

7. **Provide shortcuts for experienced users**

8. **Provide good error messages**

   Good error messages are defensive, blaming the problem on the system rather than the user; they should provide precise information about the cause of the error, and meaningful suggestions to the user about what to do next.

9. **Error prevention**

   Even better than good error messages is careful design that prevents a problem from occurring in the first place.

10.19.3 Guidelines and style guides

Where appropriate, the relevant style guide should be used to ensure a consistent interface. However, many of the *potential* problems flagged-up by the use of guidelines are not *actually* experienced by users, so guidelines tend to be rather alarmist.

10.20 Tools for interface development

Typically, the system interface accounts for around 50% of actual code, and 40-60% of application development time, so anything which raises the productivity of interface coding will have a big impact on overall development time.

Interface tools such as Visual Basic not only improve productivity, but they also help to ensure consistency of the interface through the provision of standard screen objects such as buttons, controls, dialogue boxes etc. They can also help to avoid copyright problems since the licence usually makes clear what objects can be freely copied and distributed to users.

10.20.1 Object-oriented programming and interface development

Object-oriented programming (OOP) languages contain features such as inheritance, encapsulation and polymorphism which make them particularly suitable for interface development (see Chapter 6). They allow easy construction of screen objects by the re-use of existing code, they are less likely to suffer from bugs, and the user (and programmer) doesn't have to concern themselves with the fine detail of how the code actually works. They also present visual direct-manipulation WYSIWYG development environments that better allow the developer to concentrate on the design aspects of the interface. Examples of OOP languages include C++ and Smalltalk. Languages such as Visual Basic exhibit some of the properties of OOP languages, but are event-driven rather than true OOP languages.

10.20.2 Event-driven programming

The normal status of event-driven languages is to wait for an 'event' to occur which they then process. **Events** are messages that the system or user sends to the program **objects** (menus, windows, boxes, buttons etc.). Event-driven languages are sometimes confused with OOP languages, but event-driven languages such as Visual Basic for Windows generally only offer some of the features of an OOP, for example Visual Basic offers many pre-defined classes of objects for the Windows environment, which encapsulate appropriate attributes, but it doesn't offer the same extensive class inheritance features of Smalltalk. In practice, however, such fine theoretical distinctions are likely to be relatively unimportant for the interface developer.

10.21 Evaluating the system with real users

Before we measure usability, we need to know why we're measuring it. The aim is the generation of a test plan which measures the performance of a system against acceptance criteria derived from a set of usability goals, themselves derived from an analysis of user task needs.

10.21.1 Methods of evaluation

Analytic: largely based on psychological models of user tasks, such as KLM. These can be useful for deciding which actions to provide keyboard shortcuts for.

The Keystroke Level Model measures the time taken to perform sub-tasks. Total time taken for an action is arrived at by simply adding together the times for each component task. The following table gives some timings:

Press key	
Good typist (90 wpm)	0.12 sec
Poor typist (40 wpm)	0.28 sec
Non-typist	1.20 sec
Mouse click	0.20 sec
Point with mouse	1.10 sec
Move hands to keyboard	0.40 sec

Timings for various actions in KLM (adapted from Card, Moran & Newell 1983).

Expert: Experienced systems analysts and designers evaluate the design before it is shown to end users, e.g. cognitive walkthroughs.

Observational: these can be field or usability-lab based studies of actual users of the system. They typically involve audio & video recording, verbal protocols, and data logging.

Survey: Attitude surveys, rating scales etc. are carried out with users.

Experimental: Laboratory studies to investigate different design elements.

Usability objective	Effectiveness measure	Efficiency measure	Satisfaction measure
Suitability for the task	Percentage of goals achieved	Time to complete a task	Rating scale for satisfaction
Appropriate for trained users	Number of power features used	Relative efficiency compared with an expert user	Rating scale for satisfaction with power features
Learnability	Percentage of functions learned	Time to learn criterion	Rating scale for ease of learning
Error tolerance	Percentage of errors corrected successfully	Time spent on correcting errors	Rating scale for error handling

ISO 9241 proposed software metrics (objective measures) for usability (Dix et al 1993)

10.21.2 Observation in usability labs

Studies indicate that usability testing uncovers most serious and recurring problems, and that it need not be particularly expensive, particularly if 'Discount usability testing' (Molich) is adopted, a technique which combines limited usability testing with expert evaluation.

Usability testing is especially useful for uncovering problems of interpretation, and execution errors such as problems with double-clicking a mouse.

10.22 Practical evaluation: a suggested method for those with limited time and money

- Understand the users-find some real users

- Understand the tasks-get concrete detailed examples from end users

- Produce scenarios for each sample task spelling out what actions users take and what they will see on screen. Discuss the scenarios with some real users

- Copy interaction techniques from other systems that users are familiar with, even if they aren't the most efficient

- Rough-out designs on paper; discard features that don't support any of the required tasks.

- Show paper mock-ups to a few real users

- Create a prototype, for example in Visual Basic

- Evaluate the prototype without users, using heuristics and cognitive walk-throughs. Use style guides and keystroke level modelling where appropriate

- Between 3 and 5 experienced interface experts can identify all major problems and 75% of total identifiable problems using heuristics

- Guidelines miss many severe problems, but are helpful at the design stage rather than for evaluation

- A cognitive walkthrough followed by the use of heuristics with several evaluators will catch most problems

- Test with real users and record the tests (see the summary table at the end of Chapter 8). Ensure ethical procedures are followed. De-brief the testers.

  ○ Task **process** data tells us about the hows and whys, use think aloud protocol analysis

  ○ Task **performance** data tells us how long, how many times etc.

- Repeat until specific usability acceptance criteria are met

- Use interface toolkits and prototyping systems, e.g. Motif, HyperCard, Visual Basic

- Design documentation such as manuals, training packages, on-line help and support alongside the software design. Use the 'minimal manual' approach.

Review questions

1. What is a CATWOE test, and why is it useful?

2. What diagrammatic methods are useful in analysing user requirements?

3. Describe the software design life-cycle for systems with usable inter-faces. Summarise your description with an appropriate diagram.

Test question

How should a designer go about constructing a system with a usable inter-face? Construct an annotated guideline or checklist for interface design.

Appendix Interface case study: bibliography browser

In this appendix we will work through the design of a small-scale system, putting into practice what has been covered in the rest of this book. The case study requires the design of a system to allow users who are final year higher education students to store bibliographic details of books and journal articles used for student projects and dissertations.

1. Analyse the problem situation using soft systems methodology

- Create a 'rich picture' of the problem situation
- Construct a root definition of the system.
- Apply the CATWOE test.

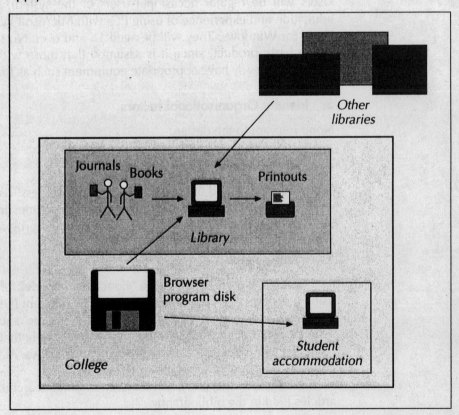

Rich Picture of problem situation

Root Definition:

'An easy to use system owned by the college and distributed to students, both with and without prior computing experience, to enable them to efficiently and effectively and with only minimal training store and retrieve bibliographic data and to print out bibliographies arranged in alphabetical order by author, on standalone IBM-PC compatible computers.'

CATWOE test:

Customers: UK Higher education institutions.

Actors: students in higher education.

Transformations: to provide computer based storage and retrieval of bibliographic data for books and journals and to print sorted bibliographies.

Weltanschauung: The system must be easy to use and require minimal training for students regardless of their prior experience of computers.

Owners: Students, HE institutions.

Environment: UK HE institutions and their libraries. UK legislation affecting computers such as the Data Protection Act, Display Screen Equipment Regulations, Copyright, Design and Patents Act etc.

2. Identify users

Users will be regular occasional users of the system, with high levels of general education and experience of using PCs with Microsoft Windows applications such as Word for Windows. They will be aged 18 and over. No special needs are catered for in the basic product, since it is assumed that those with special needs such as the blind will already have appropriate equipment such as Braille keyboards, printers etc.

3. Identify Organisational factors

None relevant to the design.

4. Identify context of use factors

The product is aimed at 'home' rather than 'business' users, and is to run on standalone machines and the college's networked machines in the library. Students are to be supplied with a floppy disk containing both the program and their data.

5. Identify tasks

At this stage, we are creating the 'Conceptual Model' of Soft Systems methodology, using a systems outline and level 0 data-flow diagram (DFD) for each task.

Check with typical end-users that all tasks are shown. This is similar to the 'Compare model and reality' stage of SSM. It is likely that there will need to be some re-design and a further iteration through earlier stages. At this stage, a user-task matrix could be constructed for multi-user systems.

Tasks include the entry, deletion, amending, searching details of the books and articles held in the bibliography.

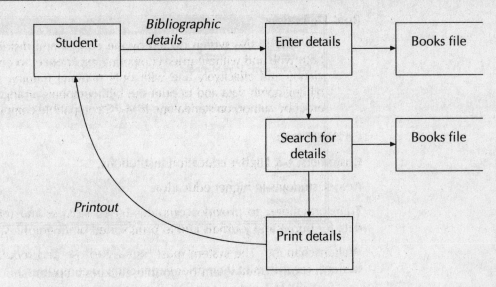

Level 0 DFD for 'Add new book or article' task

6. Decompose tasks

Produce **JSD** diagrams to show task decomposition, produce level one DFDs and entity-relationship diagrams (ERD).

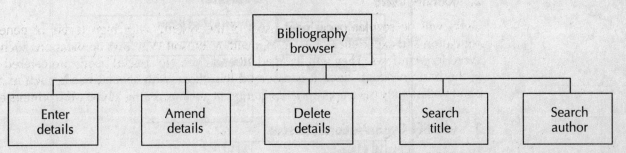

Task decomposition JSD for bibliography browser

7. Set task performance acceptance goals

State satisfactory operating criteria. Design test data plan.

- The system is to be capable of being learned by new target group users within 15 minutes and to allow tasks to be performed with no delays longer than 15 seconds. users should be able to perform each of the basic operations other than amending or adding new data in a maximum of 30 seconds 90% of the time.

- On re-using the system after a gap of one week 90% of users should be able to reach the above levels of performance within 5 minutes of first use.

8. Produce scenarios for each task

What do users do? What do they see on screen?

- The system should reside as an icon with the default name of 'Bibliography browser' in the 'Main' window.

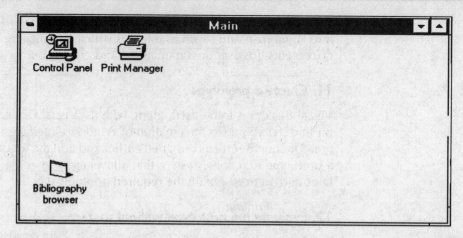

The browser icon

- On starting the system by double-clicking a screen should appear with buttons for each task option and a VCR button control to allow movement backwards and forwards through the bibliography.

Prototype part-functional browser screen for end-user evaluation

- The screen should contain standard windows elements such as close, minimise and maximise controls, and use the default standard windows colours.

9. Select technical options

The system is to be designed to run on 386-based standalone machines running Microsoft Windows 3.1 with 4Mb of RAM.

Visual Basic for Windows is to be used to create the software as it allows the creation of run-time versions that don't require additional software.

10. Produce sketches of screen design and discuss with users

Since Visual Basic is to be used, it has been decided to create screens direct in visual basic rather than producing pencil-and-paper mock-ups, since such screens can be created in next to no time with no need to build in any functionality at this stage.

Screens can be captured to the Windows Clipboard with the Print Screen key, pasted into Paintbrush and saved as bitmaps which can then be inserted into wordprocessor documents (for user documentation) and printed-out for end-user feedback.

11. Create a prototype

Visual Basic 3 is to be used, along with its 'Visual Design Guide', which provides an on-line style guide to the creation of Windows interfaces. Here we take the prototype non-functional screens designed earlier and add the required functionality, producing a prototype functional system that allows users to add and amend details, search for titles and authors, obtain the required printouts etc.

12. Evaluate the prototype without users

Applying cognitive walkthroughs, heuristics, KLM and the use of style guides/guide-lines where appropriate.

- The Visual Basic 3 Microsoft Windows style guide is to be used to achieve consis-tency with other Windows software. The software is checked by designers and preferably an outsider (to the development team) with experience of Windows interface design to assess the extent to which it complies with the Style Guide.

- Evaluators 'walkthrough' each of the tasks, using the interface screens, from the point of view of a typical user with no prior computing experience, to try to uncover potential problems.

- Common tasks which can be speeded up by the use of keyboard shortcuts are identified, using typical values from KLM analyses of typical users.

- Molich & Nielsen's Heuristics for dialogue design are used to assess the following factors:

Simplicity and naturalness of dialogues, consistency of the interface, memory load, provision of feedback e.g. when searching for authors, good screen messages, clear exits from the program and task, designing-out of errors and availability of appropriate keyboard shortcuts.

It is decided to use five evaluators with interface design experience, rather than rely on just one.

13. Re-design the prototype in the light of the above evaluation results

The evaluation revealed several shortcomings and potential problems (but remember that many of the problems identified when using style guides don't necessarily cause problems for users-heuristics are usually more reliable predictors of problems).

14. Test the new prototype with typical real users. Record test results

Here, it was decided to use 'Discount usability engineering', observing a small sample of six typical users using the software on one of the college's networked computers, and using verbal (think aloud) protocols. A test schedule was designed with hand-written bibliographic details of ten books and ten journal articles. Users were timed and after the test session were de-briefed and invited to comment on the system and to suggest shortcomings and potential improvements. One user got so frustrated that he abandoned the test session. He was carefully de-briefed to ensure that as far as possible he realised that his frustration was caused by the design of the interface, rather than any personal inadequacy on his part.

15. Repeat stages 11-14 until acceptance criteria are met

Four iterations of the design-test-evaluate-re-design cycle were undertaken until criteria were met.

16. Design documentation plan using information from stages one to four

- Getting started guide: A two-page guide to what the system does, screen appearance, starting the system, system limitations, hardware and software requirements etc.

- Minimal manual tutorial booklet based on tasks identified in stage six. The manual offers troubleshooting help for likely errors such as miss-keying.

- Quick reference card for typical tasks.

- On-line tutorial

- On-line help based on items that appear on the screens

- Help topic index. Five users who tested the system were asked to provide names for all the operations, with the index based on the results of this.

17. Establish your copyright in the system where appropriate

A copy of the original program was lodged with the designer's solicitor should any problems occur over copyright.

18. Ensure compliance with any relevant legislation or in-house rules

- Since the system stores and processes information about identifiable living people, it is necessary to register under the Data Protection Act. However, the existing college registration may cover the system. This needs to be checked with the Data Protection Registrar.

- The software is checked for compliance with the software requirements of EEC/90 Display Screen Equipment Regulations, using a checklist based on the regulations. However, since the interface has been designed with software ergonomics and usability in mind, no problems are found. Checking hardware compliance is beyond the scope of the design brief, since no hardware is to be supplied.

Answers to review questions

Chapter 1

1. It is a central concern, since the whole point of HCI is to produce effective easy to use systems.

2. The jobs that people do with computers, the operations that they perform.

3. Because there are different types of user, with different needs and characteristics.

4. Novice, expert, occasional/casual, user with special needs etc.

Chapter 2

1. Novice, occasional, expert, older, those with special needs, group workers, users working in special environments etc.

2. After observing and talking to typical end users, they can be involved in the design team. Analysts can use JSP-like diagrams to analyse and decompose tasks using task analysis techniques, and to construct user-role matrices similar to those used in SSADM. Where appropriate, KLM techniques can be used to estimate which operations benefit from keystroke shortcuts. TAG, CLG and KAT can all be used, along with more traditional systems analysis techniques such as Data Flow Diagrams. Cognitive walkthroughs try to identify possible problems and their solutions.

3. Semiotics is the science of signs, and is concerned with how we interpret the meaning of signs and symbols. Semiotics emphasises the arbitrary nature of most sign systems, and the need to take account of users perceptions of the context of use, as with the example in the text of the piggy-bank icon for save in Excel.

4. No, psychologists have shown that we tend to be easily distracted by detail and contextual features that aren't relevant to solving the problem. Humans tend to generalise from past experiences, called induction, even where such generalisations are inappropriate. This helps explain why users invariably don't follow step-by-step instructions, and no-one reads software manuals until they get stuck.

5. If we understand how the user perceives their tasks we can then make the software fit in with the user's conceptual model and behave in ways that the user will expect, rather than making the user try to fit in with the software.

6. It is only by considering organisational and sociological factors that we can appreciate just how a system is likely to be used. It is common for new systems to be supported by some groups but opposed by others, and such conflict is important for making sense of users' reactions to the software. New systems themselves

are also likely to have an impact on human factors such as power relationships in the workplace etc.

Chapter 3

1. Because they are very flexible, offer good feedback to users and are easy to use and understand. Keyboards that don't have full-travel keys, such as membrane keyboards, should be avoided where possible since they are not liked by users and reduce performance considerably, especially for experienced users.

2. Moving video requires enormous memory and processing power by current standards, and existing personal computers and local area networks can't adequately cope with these demands yet. However, developments in compression techniques and the user of wider bandwidth telecommunications facilities such as fibre optic cabling and ISDN make moving video feasible in the near future.

3. Videoconferencing systems overcome some of the non-verbal communication issues when using traditional Email systems, since they allow moving images of the participants to be displayed.

4. Speech-based control systems are relatively easy to implement, but the recognition of continuous speech is an enormous challenge since it involves digitising speech in real time, analysing the digitised speech, extracting meaning from it and producing appropriate responses. Limitations of existing telephone networks also omit speech recognition systems.

5. As with any other type of user, the key is to involve typical end-users in the design early on. There is no typical special needs user, there are lots of different groups of users with different special needs. Assumptions by those without such special needs may well be inappropriate, for example sighted users might think that speech input and output would be a major benefit for blind users, but such users may already be perfectly happy with Braille keyboards and printers and prefer them to voice recognition and speech synthesis systems.

6. Because they rely on precise memory (recall) of exact syntax of expressions, whereas menu-based systems only require the user to recognise the appropriate command. Psychologists have shown that it is much easier for humans to recognise commands than to recall them. Even the slightest syntax error in a command interface, such as an additional space, or the use of upper instead of lower case, can cause errors.

Chapter 4

1. ISO 9241, which is in 17 parts and is still being developed. The earlier parts have already been incorporated within the older BS 7169 standard, and cover mainly hardware. Later parts cover software ergonomics. BS 7649 is concerned with the documentation for software applications, and is discussed in chapter seven. The Display Screen Equipment Regulations EEC 90/270, which came into force on 1 January 1994 are also concerned with both hardware and software ergonomics, and cover employees and self-employed and contract workers who use computer workstations.

2. These are covered by EEC 90/270 and include the assessment of risk, regular audits of the safety aspects of VDU workstations, visual problems such as flicker, glare, eyestrain, headaches etc. Posture problems such as back and neck pains, adequate space to work and rest arms etc., keyboard related problems such as

work-related upper limb disorders (WRULDS), the best-known of which is Repetitive Strain Injury (RSI), VDU emissions, the provision of sight tests and glasses where necessary for VDU work, the use of software to monitor work rates, and general usability of software. More general health and safety at work issues are covered in the Management of Health and Safety at Work Act 1992, which implements EU directives on workplace health and safety.

3. As well as the health and safety issues covered in the previous question, designers must pay particular attention to the requirements of the Data Protection Act where the data stored concerns identifiable living individuals, the Copyright Design and patents Act which covers copyright, licensing, code distribution etc. issues, the Computer Misuse Act, which covers hacking. Additionally, where the software is to be used outside the UK the relevant legislation in other countries needs to be considered, and is likely to differ substantially from the UK.

Chapter 5

1. Because in those days processing power limited displays to text only, and VDUs were by no means standard. Systems tended to be used by intensive users, with little if any casual use, so it was worthwhile training individuals to use the system. Many systems of this era were batch systems rather than the interactive on-line systems typical today, which further reduced the need to consider interface issues to the same extent.

2. Usually because of poor requirements analysis and or poor logical design. Insufficient use of typical end-users early in the life-cycle are the most common causes of such poor analysis and design.

3. SSADM is the official UK government method for large systems (over £100,000 and one person-year) development, and is required by contractors working on such large scale systems. It is currently at version four, and has separate interface design stages, although these tend to be limited to advice to incorporate any appropriate style guides, rather than containing a full interface design method.

4. Formal methods aim to take a program specification and prove that it will execute correctly. As such, they are not concerned with interface issues as such and are based on deductive reasoning. However, real users make mistakes, which can cause unpredictable effects.

5. Because both methods emphasise the understanding of the problem situation and the need to involve typical end-users at the beginning of the development process, and to involve them as members of the design team in the case of Participative design methods.

Chapter 6

1. Task analysis is concerned with the observation and analysis of user behaviour in realistic contexts, whereas cognitive modelling approaches such as GOMS etc. assume error-free expert performance and don't observe real users.

2. Participative design methods such as ETHICS ensure that real user needs are incorporated in the design by making such users part of the design team. Generally speaking, the greater the degree of user involvement, the more likely that most user needs will be taken into consideration.

3. Guidelines often conflict with each other and predict problems which don't occur in real life. Style guides are product specific guidelines, such as the Microsoft Windows style guide, and tell designers how to achieve consistent interfaces in that particular environment. Heuristics are general rules of thumb rather than detailed guidelines, and have been found to produce good usable interface designs and to be better tools than guidelines.

4. OOP development tools allow modular program design and code re-use, which are sound software engineering practices resulting in more reliable programs. They are particularly suited to the design of interactive direct manipulation environments as a result of the use of encapsulation, inheritance and polymorphism. Event driven languages such as Visual Basic possess some of the features of Object-Oriented languages.

Chapter 7

1. Basically, a usable interface is one which is easy to learn, allows efficient performance and is comfortable to use.

2. The experimental situation is artificial and unrealistic, so we can't really generalise to real life situations except in very limited circumstances.

3. See section 7.5 The user needs analysis allows us to identify the usability goals of our system. We can then test the system to see if these goals are met.

4. Quantitative data is concerned with numeric measurement, e.g. of number of tasks completed, number of times help is used etc., whereas qualitative data is more concerned with an in-depth understanding of the reasons for something, for example, understanding why a user makes a particular error.

5. Metrics are objective evaluation criteria such as time taken to complete a task, number of errors made etc.

Chapter 8

1. Metrics are objective evaluation criteria such as time taken to complete a task etc.

2. See the section on Molich's heuristics

3. A separate test room, designed to look like a typical office environment, with an observation room and one-way glass and a video camera to record the users.

4. By using a Likert 5 or 7 point attitude scale.

5. Where the problem is very simple with few if any variables affecting performance, for example, to measure the time taken to perform a particular set of actions with a mouse compared with using the keyboard.

Chapter 9

1. Avoid short-term memory load, allow for technophobia, anticipate that users will read everything first before starting to use the system.

2. They are good for getting the look and feel of an interface, and if users are required to perform the task once only, but poor for longer term performance compared to written manuals.

3. Reduce verbiage, layout is user-task based rather than program function based, anticipate mistakes and provide information on how to recover from common errors.

4. See the section on BS 7649

5. How do I do a particular operation?, what does this operation do?, how did this happen, how do I get out of it?, whereabouts am I and how do I get back to the main menu/screen etc.

6. Alongside software development, using the same approach of iterative development with prototyping.

Chapter 10

1. Customers, Actors, Transformations, Weltanschauung, Owners, Environment

2. Data flow diagrams

3. The star life-cycle, with development starting at many possible different points.

Bibiography and further reading

Avison & Wood-Harper, *Multiview*, Blackwell 1990

Bennett, Case, Sandelin, Smith, *Visual Display Terminals: Usability issues and health concerns*, 1984 Prentice-Hall

Bevan & Macleod, 'Usability measurement in context', *Behaviour & Information Technology* 1994 v13, 1&2

Carroll, *The Nurnberg Funnel*, MIT 1990

Checkland, *Systems Thinking, Systems Practice*, Wiley 1981

Dix, Finlay, Abowd, Beale, *Human-Computer Interaction*, Prentice-Hall 1993

Downs, Clare & Coe, *SSADM*, 2nd edition, Prentice-Hall 1992

Gould & Lewis, 'Designing for Usability: Key Principles and What Designers Think', *Communications of the ACM* 28 1985

Johnson, *Human-Computer Interaction*, McGraw-Hill 1992

Molich & Nielsen, 'Improving a Human-Computer Dialogue', *Communications of the ACM*, 1990, v33, 3

Preece, Rogers, Sharp, Benyon et al, *Human-Computer Interaction*, Adison-Wesley 1994

Robson, *Experiment, Design and Statistics in Psychology*, Penguin 1983

Shackel, 'The Concept of Usability', in Bennett et al, *Visual Display Terminals*, 1984 op cit

Walsham, *Interpreting Information Systems in Organisations*, Wiley 1993

Yourdon & Constantine, *Structured Design*, 4th edition, Yourdon Press 1979

In addition to the above books, *PC Magazine*, produced monthly by Ziff-Davis publishers, evaluate usability of a group of software products each month, using typical end-users in their own usability lab and employing a human factors specialist usability editor.

Index

Analytic Evaluation Methods, 109
Animated Demonstrations , 153
Apple Macintosh, 9,100

BS 7649: Design Of Documentation , 51, 141

CD-ROM Devices, 34, 40
Claims Analysis And Stakeholders, 15, 129
CLG, 113
Co-operative Evaluation., 128
Cognitive Complexity Theory (CCT), 112
Cognitive Walkthrough, 120
Colour Perception, 17
Command Language Grammar (CLG), 113
Command-Language Interfaces, 41
COMPACT, 75
Computer Misuse Act 1990-Computer Hacking, 60
Conceptual Modelling, 22, 88
Conformance Testing Of Software, 58
Context Of Use, 25, 159
Context-Sensitive Help, 149
Contextual inquiry, 129
CSCW, 14
Copyright Law And The Interface, 58
Cue Cards, 147

Data flow diagrams, 107, 171
Data Protection Act 1984, 60
DIADEM, 72
Dialogues, 5
Direct Manipulation, 7, 45
Display Screen Equipment Regulations EEC 90/270, 52
Document Types And Their Use, 144
Documentation, 157
Documentation Writing Style, 141, 145

Emoticons, 18
Ergonomic Standards, 49, 52
ETHICS, 78
Ethical Issues In Testing, 108
Ethnography, 24, 129
Evaluation methods, 133, 164, 166
Event-Driven Programming, 99
Experimental Evaluation, 116-119
Expert Evaluation Methods, 119
Expert users, 12

Form-Fill, 44
Full-Motion Video In Training Materials, 153-154

GOMS, 110
Group Workers & CSCW, 14, 90

Guidelines, 92, 121

HCI, 1
HCI And The Software Life Cycle, 8, 63
Health & Safety At Work: General Requirements, 52
Help systems, 46
Heuristics, 94
HUFIT, 73
Human Factors Guidelines, 73
Human Perception, 15
HUSAT , 72
HyperCard , 100
Hypermedia and Hypertext Help Systems, 150

Icons, 17
Indexes, 148
Input Devices, 27
Installation Instructions, 146
Intelligent' Help Systems, 150
Interaction Styles, 5, 160
International HCI Standards:, 48
ISO 9241, 49
Iterative Design And Prototyping, 71, 173

Jackson Structured Programming/Design (JSP/JSD), 82, 171
KAT (Knowledge Analysis Of Tasks)., 115
Keyboards, 28
Keystroke Level Model (KLM), 111

Legal Issues When Distributing Systems, 58

Memory, 19
Menus, 42
Metaphors And Conceptual Models, 22
Minimalist Instruction, 137-141
Motif And X-Windows, 99
Motivation, 25
MULTIVIEW, 79

Natural Language Dialogue, 43
Non-Keyboard Input, 30
Novice Users, 12

Object-Oriented Programming And Interface Development., 96
Observational Methods Of Evaluation, 125
Occasional Users, 12
Older Users, 13, 153
On-Line Help, 46, 148
Organisational Factors, 7, 91
Output Devices, 38

Participative Design, 77
Practical Evaluation, 131, 167

Prototyping, 71, 173

Question And Answer dialogues, 44
Quick Reference Materials, 147

Reasoning, 20
Representing Users' Knowledge , 88, 102, 106
Semiotics And Icons, 17

Smalltalk, 97
Social aspects of HCI, 23
Soft Systems Methodology (SSM), 74, 162, 169
Software Ergonomics, 156
Software Ergonomics Requirements Of EEC 90/270, 57
Software Licensing, 59
Software Life-Cycle And Interface Design, 8, 63
Software Piracy, 59
Sound, 41
Speech, 35-38
SSADM, 67
Star Life-cycle Model, 84, 163
Structured Methods, 64
Style guides, 92
Support On The Internet, 152
Supporting Design, 101
Survey Based Evaluation, 130

Task Action Grammar (TAG), 115
Task Action Language (TAL), 114
Task Analysis, 87, 105
Tasks, 4, 105, 141
Telephone Support, 152, 158
Tools For Interface Development, 96, 165
Training Materials, 46, 158
Tutorials, 146

Usability, 3, 57, 103, 125
Usability engineering, 126
Usability labs, 125, 128
Usability metrics, 126
User Motivations, 25
User Needs Analysis, 89, 105
User Software Engineering (USE), 83
Users, 3, 11, 105, 141
Users With Special Needs, 14

Video, 34, 153
Videoconferencing, 35
Virtual Reality Headsets, 41
Visual Basic For Windows, 100, 172
Visual Display Units (VDUs), 38
Writing Documentation For Software., 141
WRULDS, 30

X-windows, 99

Operating Systems

C Ritchie

Level: HND/Degree **Series:** In a Semester

It is known to be used on the following courses: BTEC Higher National, first and second year Computing degree courses, Software Engineering and Mechanical Engineering degrees. It is on the reading list of IDPM.

The new edition, apart from a general update, incorporates a significant amount of detail on PC Windowing systems, including newer technologies such as DDE, OLE and ODBC.

Review comments

'This is one of the most exciting, useful and lucid books on the subject I have seen.' 'Excellent – I wish I had had it when I was a student.' 'Very readable book with difficult concepts presented in a clear, understandable way.' Lecturers

2nd edition • 240 pp • Feb 1995 • ISBN 1 85805 131 2

Local Area Networks

P Hodson

Level: HND/Degree **Series:** In a Semester

It is known to be used on the following courses: IDPM, BTEC Higher National Computing and Computing degree courses.

The new edition, in addition to a general update, includes an introductory data communications section.

Review comments

'There is no other book that covers these technical aspects with this clarity.' 'Easy to follow and understand.' 'Excellent value for money.' 'Contents of the book excellent. It will surely be on my reading list. Worth so much more than its cover price!' 'Excellent value and detailed coverage of the topic.' Lecturers

2nd edition • 240 pp • April 1995 • ISBN 1 85805 133 9

Programming with ANSI C

B J Holmes

Level: HND/Degree **Series:** Complete Course Text

This book comprehensively covers the official standard version (American National Standards Institute) of the programming language C and assumes the reader has no prior experience of other computer languages.

Contents: Programming environment, Data, Input and output, Instruction sequence, Selection, Repetition, Functions, Macros and mathematics, One-dimensional arrays, Arrays and structures, Pointers, Program development, Recursion, Sorting and searching, Files, Lists and trees, Further topics.

Note: All the programs have been written in ANSI C and as a result may be run in either MS-DOS or UNIX environments.

1st edition • 528 pp • June 1995 • ISBN 1 85805 117 7

Convert to C and C^{++}

B J Holmes

Level: HND/Degree **Series:** Complete Course Text

This book is known to be used on the following courses: BTEC Higher National Computing, BA Computing, MSc Computing and Information Systems, City & Guilds 726.

Review Comments

'Excellent book. Wide range of language covered, well presented and at a very reasonable price.'
'Excellent price, good coverage, straightforward and readable.' Lecturers

1st edition • 320 pp • 1992 • ISBN 1 873981 20 1

Programming in Visual Basic

P K MacBride

Level: HND/Degree **Series:** Complete Course Text

The book is suitable for use with versions 2.0 and 3.0. It is known to be used on C & G, GNVQ Advanced, ALC, BTEC National.

Contents: Designing and creating programs, Program flow, Interacting with the user, Testing and debugging, Graphics, Procedures, functions and forms, Arrays, Sequential files, Records and random access files, MDI Forms.

Review comments

'Definitely an answer to prayer!' 'So much easier to learn from than a manual!' 'Excellent book at a good price.' 'A must for all students of Visual Basic.' 'An excellent book at an affordable price.'   Lecturers

1st edition • 208 pp • Sept 1994 • ISBN 1 85805 092 8